"As a specialist IT law... in private practice a... from start-ups to large multi-nationals, I have seen the very best and the very worst of sales performances. In Jim's book I have found countless echoes of my own experiences and commercial encounters. I found myself nodding in agreement on almost every page. This book will be of great value to any salesperson at any stage of their careers - excellent advice for the beginner, and a timely aide-memoire for the experienced. I commend it."

Paul Klinger LLB, Solicitor. Former Director of Legal Services, EMEA, at Silicon Graphics, Inc.

The B2B Selling Guidebook

Powerful tips, techniques and tools to help you succeed in Business-to-Business (B2B) selling – based on over 40 years of real-world experience, testing and on-the-job research.

Jim Irving

The B2B Selling Guidebook
First edition - 2020 by Jim Irving, distributed
in partnership with ebookpartnership.com
Copyright © Jim Irving 2020.

ISBN 9781672330954

The right of Jim Irving to be identified as
the author of this work has been asserted in
accordance with sections 77 and 78 of the
Copyright, Designs and Patents Act 1988.

All rights reserved. No part of this book may
be reproduced in any form or by any electronic
or mechanical means, including information
storage and retrieval systems without the
specific written permission of the author.
Short excerpts may be quoted, but only for
the purposes of press coverage, reviews or
interviews and must be credited to the author.

The stories told in "The B2B Selling Guidebook"
are for illustrative purposes only. Specific
stories, individual names, locations and
products or services have been modified
or amended as necessary to maintain
confidentiality. No identification of actual
individuals (living or dead), organisations,
locations, products and services is intended,
made or should be inferred.

This book is available in e-book, paperback
and audiobook formats.

Design by weareseventhree.com

Compendium
noun /kəmˈpen.di.əm/

A detailed collection of information on a particular subject, especially in a short book...

Source: MacMillan Dictionary

About the Author

Jim was born in Edinburgh, Scotland and now lives in rural Northern Ireland with his wife, Yvonne. He has spent over 43 years in Business to Business (B2B) selling with a number of industry leading technology organisations including Amdahl, Sequent, Silicon Graphics (SGI) and Information Builders (www.ibi.com).

His career started with the hardest possible assignment - selling office equipment door to door in Scotland, in the depths of winter! His career rapidly developed into senior selling and sales leadership roles then ultimately to senior executive positions at major multinationals – including becoming the UK MD of Information Builders – a leading US based enterprise software company. At Silicon Graphics he was awarded the Corporation's 'Exemplary Leader' award. Jim has also held several executive marketing posts. For the last 14 years he has run his own consulting business helping start-ups to improve their B2B strategy and selling results. He has advised and helped many start-ups to better execute and grow their businesses.

Jim has travelled extensively and worked worldwide. He gained an MBA from Edinburgh Napier University in 1988. He is a Fellow of both the Chartered Institute of Marketing and The Institute of Sales Management. He has spoken at a number of seminars and conferences and has in the past been an occasional visiting lecturer to both the MBA school at Edinburgh Napier University and to the Postgraduate Business School at Queens University, Belfast.

When not working, Jim enjoys dining out, family time, the gym, travel, reading fiction and following current affairs.

"The selling process offers a peep-hole into the human condition. In this book, Jim helps the sales person see reality, develop insights and then, most of all, add long-term value to the client-supplier relationship."

Bob Bishop, Former Chairman & CEO, Silicon Graphics Inc.

"Jim's reputation is very well established. He has gone in to lead sales/the business in difficult circumstances and markets and has delivered clarity in strategy and also in sales execution and improved results. He understands the dynamics of selling."

Professor Paul Atkinson, Founding Partner - Par Equity (a multi award winning VC firm), Executive Chairman Taranata Group and serial investor.

"His no-frills, straightforward and ethical approach to building a world-class sales organization is something to this day that I not only admire, but also strive to emulate."

David Rode, Former Senior Vice President, International Operations, Information Builders Inc. (IBI)

"I first met Jim when I asked him to be the MD of a technology company I chaired. He brought clarity and strong execution to the business and massively increased market visibility while improving business results and motivating staff. He delivers very strong sales and communication skills to every endeavour"

Michael Black MBE, Successful technology entrepreneur. Non-Executive Director at Danske Bank, Non-Executive Director at Titan IC Systems and Chairman – Displaynote Technologies

"Jim is one of those few people who has a real presence... This credible presence and his great persuading and influencing skills are invaluable when communicating at the highest levels within the organisation..."

Chief Data Officer, UK Top 3 FTSE Company

"A key objective for any company is revenue growth. Jim Irving is one of the select band of individuals with a long track record of making a real difference where it matters most - the bottom line."

Jim Green, CEO and Co-Founder, Spartan Solutions

"As a specialist IT lawyer with over 40 years' experience both in private practice and in-house, I have acted for IT businesses from start-ups to large multi-nationals. I have seen the very best and the very worst of sales performances. In Jim's book I have found countless echoes of my own experiences and commercial encounters. I found myself nodding in agreement on almost every page. This book will be of great value to any salesperson at any stage of their careers - excellent advice for the beginner, and a timely aide-memoire for the experienced. I commend it."

Paul Klinger LLB, Solicitor. Former Director of Legal Services, EMEA, at Silicon Graphics, Inc.

"The most difficult challenge in business is to make simplicity out of complexity. Jim is one of those few who can make any process seem simple. His methodical and diligent approach to the sales process and every sales cycle is why he has seen and passed on so much success."

Ryan McAnlis, Former CEO, JAR Technologies

"Jim is a natural sales leader, able to instantly command attention and respect from both his sales team and prospective clients. He has a relaxed and friendly approach which puts customers at ease and gains their trust. This, coupled with a keen commercial drive, enables him to identify opportunity, develop winning sales arguments and effectively manage the sales process to ensure his team make their numbers."

Ian Baxter, Vice President - NetDimensions

"Jim is a seasoned sales leader with a proven track record of success in multiple channels and business models. His leadership and motivation skills elevate the productivity of his teams resulting in consistently exceeded goals. He is respected by his customers, team, peers, and senior management."

Greg Goelz, President & CEO, Smart Locus Inc, California

For Yvonne, the world's best proof reader!
And my wonderful children and grandchildren. Also,
for my brother Mike and sister Pat - 'gone too soon'.

Look out for the follow up book

...coming later in 2020!

Introduction

"Experience is the best teacher."

Penelope Douglas, Author

Purpose
This book is not about theory! Rather, it represents the culmination of well over 40 years spent at the coal face of B2B (aka enterprise) Selling. Over that time, I have made many mistakes – but I have learnt from them. Today, as I run my consulting business, I see the same mistakes being repeated everywhere I travel. I want to share my experience in order to help those who follow to close more business, sell better and smarter and accelerate their careers. This book is not a 'Guide to Everything About Selling'. Nor is it a formal or rigid methodology. It simply highlights a number of approaches, tactics and processes I have used to achieve greater success in the real world and that can be universally applied.

Audience
The book is designed to help those who are interested in selling B2B (Business to Business). It will also be of use to those who sell directly to consumers (B2C) and marketing, finance, 'C' Suite, support and legal professionals who 'touch' the world of sales. The book will deliver the greatest and most direct help to those who sell (or want to sell) high value products, services, professional services, consulting, projects and solutions regardless of the marketplace. If you work for/sell for a start-up, a mid-sized organisation or a large corporation these principles apply equally to you. Why? Everyone sells! Whether it's influencing your boss or a business partner, or 'pitching' an idea, it's part of life. My own direct experience is in Enterprise Hardware, Software, Consulting and Services but the principles are truly universal. I assume throughout that, at a minimum, you have a desire to learn more about B2B selling approaches, skills and techniques.

Format
The format is very simple. This is not a textbook, it's more of a compendium. Each concept has its own short, discrete chapter. Each chapter introduces the concept, gives a real-world example or two, then finally summarises the learning

and suggests things to try. I have written the book to be light, short, conversational and easy to follow. My goal in each case was that my wife, Yvonne – a Doctor with no commercial experience – could read and easily understand each sales principle and message. I hope I have succeeded. The book is designed to be dipped into, with each chapter delivering specific learning and value.

Experience
I joined the nascent technology sector when it was in its infancy. The sector is challenging but can be very rewarding – a great choice in retrospect! I have been fortunate to work with some of the world's greatest technology companies, names that have effectively helped to create the world in which we now live. I have always, through timing and coincidence, ended up working for the Number two or three company in the sectors I have worked in – I have never worked for the de facto largest, market leader. This has meant that for over 40 years I have been fighting big battles for large scale deals and relationships, but always as the contender, not the dominant market force. This in turn has meant that I have always had to work harder and smarter in order to succeed. I have lost at the end of long campaigns, but always then tried to learn from that experience - and I have won a lot of business too. Enough to win many sales awards, rewards trips and recognition over the years. Selling has been my life and I hope it can be a long-term success for you too.

Value
I strongly believe that those who read and then adopt the principles and tactics in this book will achieve higher revenue numbers/margins and stand out from both colleagues and competitors in their marketplace. This is not a traditional sales manual that delivers a complete outline list of 'The perfect process' or 'Everything you need to do, step by step'. It is an easy-to-read sample of some of the most powerful tools, tips and techniques that have really worked for me and which will give you an edge over your competition.

Stories
All of the stories in this book are real. BUT, to save the innocent and protect the guilty I have changed the place, name, company name, company type, geography and marketplace details in every case. ☺

Credits and Acknowledgements
Over the last 43 years, I have worked under some of the best managers and leaders in the world, I have had fantastic sales training (formal and on the job) and experienced consistent and grinding competition against the leading players in my field. This book reflects all that I have learned from these sources. There are too many mentors, competitors and friends to name individually but, as you read the stories, you may well see yourself in there! I thank you all for the lifetime of experience – both good and bad – that has enabled me to deliver this mini compendium.

I would also like to thank all of those who helped to bring this work to life. Those who proofed it, assisted my memory (!), who added insight, clarity and those who provided supporting quotes. Your help was invaluable and very much appreciated. You know who you are. 43 years is a very long time so where I have remembered something, or the original source, incorrectly, the fault is 100% mine.

"I am still learning..."

Michelangelo

Contents

Chapter 1	Service Led Selling	14
Chapter 2	Selling Strategically - 'Outside the Box'	20
Chapter 3	"Are You Lazy or Just Stupid?"	25
Chapter 4	Follow the Numbers	31
Chapter 5	Friends and Enemies – Political Selling	39
Chapter 6	The B2B Switch Sell	46
Chapter 7	Ask the Dumb Questions!	52
Chapter 8	Really Understand the Target Organisation	57
Chapter 9	Don't Forget the Board (and Others)	63
Chapter 10	Keep the Competition Busy	68
Chapter 11	Care... But Not Too Much	73
Chapter 12	Qualification	78
Chapter 13	What is Real Value?	84
Chapter 14	Competition	91
Chapter 15	Attitude in Your Business Life	98
Chapter 16	Leading From the Front	105
Chapter 17	Selling in the World of Subscription Pricing	110
Chapter 18	Negotiation	116
Chapter 19	Focus On Your Priorities	123
Chapter 20	Attitude in Your Personal Life	128
Chapter 21	Summary and Conclusion	136
Appendix 1	**Quotes About the Author** – full versions of the quotes summarised in the introduction, plus additional quotes	140
Appendix 2	**Resources** – books, information sources and other materials that might be useful to you	143
Appendix 3	A Sample Sales Process and 'Ratios' Form	146
Appendix 4	**Some More Words** – about the theories and individuals quoted in the book	151

Chapter 1
Service Led Selling

"Do not follow where the path may lead. Go instead where there is no path and leave a trail."

Harold R McAlindon

Introduction

I was recently in the market for a new car – just a small 'run around' to replace a larger, older and less efficient car – doing my bit for the planet. I looked at three options which were all very close in specification. In each case I took a test drive and then said I would think about it. All three salesmen (and in this case they were all men) seemed professional and competent. I was a real buyer... I had cash and motive... I was really interested in their products and told them so... Now five months on, not one has followed up to see what I was doing. Such a shame and also such a lost opportunity for each of them. If just one had followed up and truly been interested, they would almost certainly have their commission now. Has that happened to you in your personal life? How do you feel when a salesperson lets you down? This 'poor service – v - fantastic service' feeling in a customer can be enormously useful to you in B2B selling. The simple fact is that salespeople often commit and promise to do, more than they actually deliver. A lot is said, but less is done...

An Example

I was trying to break into a critical target account in Manufacturing. I was, as we all often are, hitting my head against the proverbial brick wall. Nothing seemed to have been working. But I had obviously done just enough to get noticed as I was then invited to compete with their incumbent supplier for the next large deal, which was really important to their business success – a truly strategic procurement for the customer. I had built an effective network of friends and contacts, both in the sector and in the local market and I heard through my grapevine that the incumbent supplier was totally unconcerned about our presence. They had a multi-year joint history, a great ongoing working relationship, good technology and a couple of staff deeply embedded (full time) with the customer. Thinking back, I guess if I was them, I would have been pretty confident too!

I racked my brains but could not think of any traditional way to win the deal and the customer relationship going forward. Then I decided I would try what I later termed 'Service Led Selling'. (Note: not Services Led, which is another thing entirely...) It was an initial, fairly unscientific attempt to win over the customer by contrasting their experience with us and with their incumbent. Luckily the prospect was a large, traditional organisation with a methodical approach to the buying process and with a lot of their people wanting answers to a large number of questions.

The tactic was very simple. We cleared a whiteboard in the office and I and the pre-sales team agreed a headline which read... *"Every request will be answered the same day"*. As the questions flowed in, we 'crawled over broken glass' to ensure that, no matter how difficult, we always got at least the basis of an answer back to them before midnight that same day. And we openly and honestly answered every question. When we simply didn't know the answer AND couldn't get it before the end of the day we still responded, explained what we did know, what action we had taken to answer their question and when we would be back to them with a definitive answer. We recorded them all on the whiteboard to ensure none were missed. It was HARD work for everyone. At one point we even figured out that the customer had perhaps guessed what we were trying to do as a lot of difficult questions seemed to come in around 5pm! But we persevered. We did this without fail throughout the length of the four to five-month campaign. Of course, at the same time we were doing our traditional sales job - needs analysis, problem solving, running presentations, speaking to their technical staff and executives and building our proposal – all the normal big-ticket sales activities. (BTW, have a look at chapter 16 for some thoughts on leading a team from the front internally).

On decision day we found that we had won the deal – and the account - outright. The incumbent was beyond shocked. One of their flagship accounts was gone and they just couldn't figure out how it had happened. Had they perhaps taken their customer too much for granted? Over time as we got to know our new customer, we kept on hearing the same phrase – *"From the beginning we just felt we could trust you more to deliver this critical project".* The constant drip, drip, drip of us responding quickly, fully, honestly and effectively to every request, compared with the normal approach from a big vendor – answering questions in a few days or so, not answering everything fully (particularly if a truthful answer didn't look good), sometimes completely missing out the answers that were not positive – had created a powerful impression and impact. Psychology talks about the fact that 'negativity bias' (your bad feelings towards something caused through bad experience) is actually stronger than the equivalent 'positivity bias'. So, if one vendor is constantly reinforcing a negative experience and the other is reinforcing positive actions and attitude, then you subconsciously start to see a big gap between them. But, putting aside the psychology theory, all I know is that it worked very well for me!

I would love to be able to say that I have done this religiously on every major deal since then, but that just wouldn't be anywhere near true. HOWEVER, on those once in a while, highest-level, critical deals AND assuming you have a team that will truly agree with the idea and actively support you, this tactic can have an amazing impact on the customer relationship and trust.

The Lesson
Hard work pays off. Hard, consistent, detailed work pays even better... If all else is equal, then being a more responsive supplier, with a more open attitude, greater consistency and a much faster response time will directly, although subliminally, impact on the individuals you deal with. They will 'just feel' you are a better bet for them. Put simply, if you continue to do the right things, then the right things will happen. A warning however, you can't ever 'half

do' this. Starting out to work in this way and then dropping off your effort will have the exact opposite effect; they will become increasingly disappointed in you. *"We thought at first you were better than that..."* James Muir describes selling as *"A sample of how you solve..."* and that is what we are doing here. Service Led Selling is a fantastic tool to keep up your sleeve for when it's needed...

"Once you have the commitment, you need the discipline and hard work to get you there."

Haile Gebrselassie

Notes

Chapter 2

Selling Strategically 'Outside the Box'

"Those who let things happen usually lose to those who make things happen."

Dave Weinbaum

Introduction

You have a massive opportunity in your pipeline. You are excited about it. Winning it could make your year! But losing it would massively impact your chances of meeting your target. You already know who your core contacts are and who you still have to target, you also know what the end solution is likely to look like. We have all been there. So, what else can you do to impact your chances of winning?

<u>The concept of selling strategically means, in a very real sense, looking outside of your own 'box'.</u>

An Example

I was selling into what was then the largest potential deal of my career (seven figures, many years ago). I was one of four potential providers for just half of what the prospective customer needed to buy. Neither my company, or our three competitors, delivered any solutions in the other half (we four were all high-end enterprise <u>hardware</u> B2B vendors, the other element of the deal was complex enterprise <u>software</u> which none of us sold). The healthcare organisation – a massive, highly regarded and VERY professional buyer – had decided to choose their software first, then to look at the hardware after. Those of us that they had shortlisted for the hardware element were all told to wait until we were contacted.

On reflection, I decided to take a gamble and run a full sales campaign to all of the shortlisted software vendors. It turned out, by coincidence, there were four of them too, selling not in competition, but in parallel to the hardware vendors like us. We were not a threat or danger to each other. I reached out and made contact with each of them, sold their sales bid team our offering and its uniques and how it could help them, found mutual references that had already worked well – anywhere in the world – got quotes from those joint customers and even organised calls with them if the software supplier agreed. This was not easy; it took a lot of time and effort and I was criticised internally for *"Wasting time outside the sale"*. I soon realised that I was the only hardware supplier taking this approach, so I doubled down again. In effect, I wanted to get a 'sale' from each of the other players in the game that I could influence. They needed to know how working with us could aid their own sales campaigns...

Come the day that the RFP said we were to be contacted by the end user organisation I duly received a call. I was up against a very strong, leading incumbent and two other major industry players and was still not sure we really had a chance (we were, by far, the smallest bidder). My primary contact started laughing as she spoke to me... She said *"Well, we knew you had some reasonable technology, but we absolutely didn't expect every one of the software vendors to recommend you specifically in their proposals. Would you like to come in before the other hardware vendors - including the incumbent – to move things forward?"* You don't have to guess my answer! And three months later not only did I win the deal, which was even bigger than anticipated, but the mutual trust level from the process was by then so high they asked me if I would help them to source and then negotiate another large piece of technology for them (not directly linked to the original project). I dealt with those prospective vendors as the customer's buying agent and that deal also passed through our books with some 'rather pleasant' profit margin attached. I had stumbled on additional, hidden value in this deal. A mutually beneficial long-term relationship then ensued. All because of that first 'outside of the box' thinking. Those software vendors had acted as my partners and that collaborative approach worked well.

The Lesson
Here, the message was very clear to me. As you look at those big, strategic deals, ALWAYS look to see who else could be involved in any way – other connected (non-competing) vendors, existing suppliers, external influencers, consultants, advisors, the end users/consumers of what you deliver inside the organisation themselves. Then sit down and work out how you could reach them, influence them and, at the very worst, ensure they are neutral to what you will be doing. If you can find synergy or mutual benefit, then so much the better for both parties. I have used this approach on every critical deal I have been bidding for since then. Does it always work? Of course not. But does it increase your chances of winning – yes, every time.

"Your mind is the fuel, but creative thinking will really get you flying."

Roni Rosenthal

Notes

Chapter 3
"Are You Lazy or Just Stupid?"

"There are no secrets to success. It is the result of preparation, hard work and learning from failure."

Colin Powell

Introduction
Say the phrase 'Time Management' and most people sigh. *"Of course, we need to manage our time they say. We get it!"* But do we, really? It's also a truism that time management is critical to success in your working day. However, our world is now more packed with distractions than every generation before us has coped with, added together. Recent research points to this generation as having the shortest attention span of any since measurement began – and we can all see the reasons why. TV (with how many channels?), entertainment on demand (YouTube, Netflix et al), social media in all its guises, gaming, messaging apps, enticing websites for online entertainment, gambling and shopping, multi-media services, the power of the web itself. We are drowning in distraction, and trust me, I include myself here. My 30-year-old self would not believe how I spend my time these days.

An Example
Some people just REALLY get this. Long before all these above distractions added to the issue, one of my early bosses ran a very tight, hard ship. The sales team worked from an office in the basement of our branch operation. We had to record all of our different activities each day on a sheet of paper and total them up. About one day in three, we would hear the shout – just as the clock touched 5pm. *"Come on up and bring your sheets".* These sheets recorded everything – cold phone calls made, successful calls, follow up calls, meetings, demonstrations etc.

We would stand in a line in front of his desk. After some general chat he would pick one person each time and the routine went like this...

"Irving, let me see your sheet". Of course, if chosen, your insides fell. He then read the sheet – and I very quickly found out that he had a fantastic calculating and analytic brain.

"So, Irving, you made 48 calls today – quite good. Of those you had six meaningful conversations. Well done – a good conversion ratio. Oh, and you did one demonstration in the demo room upstairs. That all sounds good, but hold on... 48 cold calls at say just over a minute each gives me around an hour. Six conversations at around ten minutes each gives me another hour. And a demonstration takes around an hour too. But let's be kind and say yours took a total of 1.5 hours. That adds up to 3.5 hours. So, now tell me what EXACTLY did you do for the rest of the day?" At this point the poor chosen 'victim of the day' knew that whatever they said they couldn't fully account for their time.

You felt that you had worked hard, you know you were busy, but somehow you could never explain that time. Of course, in reality things always took a little longer, you muddled around on unimportant tasks and the sales team chatted throughout the day. But the principle of focus and time management was hammered into us around once or twice a week without fail.

The conversation always ended the same way. *"So, Irving, you don't know what you did today. You wasted your time. Are you lazy or just stupid?"* And he forced you to answer in front of everyone! At the time, as a new, naïve, but enthusiastic salesman, this was my worst nightmare – I am sure I woke up in the middle of the night having panic attacks about it. Looking back, I can smile and realise that a fundamental rule of good business was being forced into my brain – where it has stayed ever since. Reading this and thinking of today's business environment I guess some might say this was high pressure, perhaps almost bullying. I would strongly say the opposite. If you can't respond to and cope with pressure internally and in front of your friends and colleagues – on a subject you are actually living - how will you ever cope with difficult and demanding customers? This was good, practical teaching of a real, core business attribute and has served me well through the years.

I cannot imagine what he would say about the large corporate office of today - John on Facebook, Katie on Snapchat, Iain on YouTube, Trish catching up on the day's news, Robin doing online shopping. I think his brain would explode! But the reality is, compared with those more innocent days at the start of my career, I can only imagine the near exponential increase in wasted time. We are all busy, but are we effective? Looking back, I am so grateful that these fundamentals were given to me. It is on this foundation that my career flourished. I have been able to work more effectively, analyse how my time is used and continue to improve my performance as a result.

Today, as I meet new businesses, I am ever more concerned by the rise and rise of the 'silent sales floor' where Social Selling (or distractions) seem to have overtaken personal and physical communication. There is a place for both approaches, but you must still call, speak and meet – it's essential to the B2B sell. People still buy from people. And, on that subject here's another thing too. Every piece of sales experience and analysis tells us that the best times to call out (and get through) are between 8am and 9am and also between 4pm and 6pm. When are sales floors typically quietest with outgoing calls? Hmmm...

The Lesson
Again, don't do this for anyone else, do it for you. Seriously look at your time allocation and usage. What percent of your time in an average day is productive? I would suggest that if you can reach 50%+ you are doing much better than average. We each need to review how we can optimise our productive time and remove those distractions. Set rules for yourself. *"Online stuff only at lunchtime". "No more than 30 minutes on all social media between 0830 and 1800".* Or whatever works well for you. Stick to those maximums. In a world where your competition (internally and externally) is more and more distracted, focus, focus, focus...

"The key is in not spending time, but in investing it."

Stephen R Covey

Notes

Chapter 4

Follow the Numbers

"If you are not sure where you are going, you're liable to end up somewhere else."

Robert F Mager

Introduction

Most individuals who find their way into selling tend to be creative. We have an inherent dislike of paperwork and process. True, a lot of it seems to interfere with the real selling but we just need to do it, right? (BTW, Myers Briggs (look them up) have done great work in identifying personality types. Take their free 'instrument test' on yourself – it is very enlightening). But some process is critical to your success. What if I told you there is a form of paperwork that will help drive you to achieve greater success? And it is for you to use to help yourself? No matter what paper based or CRM system you use, there is a self-managed form of data usage that can be invaluable to you, regardless of where you are in your career. Now, this chapter is a bit more intense, so get a cup of water, juice or coffee and a nice biscuit, relax for a moment and then read on...

An Example

Right at the start of my selling career I was very lucky to be taught a lot of skills and techniques in a six-week intensive course that was famous throughout the industry for its aggression, ultra-high work requirements and even higher dropout rates. Some of what I learned has been long lost in the mists of time. But a few, just a few, principles, have stayed with me for over 40 years. This is one of them. And it is fantastic...

Let's assume you are working in a new business environment and you own your whole sales cycle – a very common situation. You have to do the research, the cold calling/first contact, the follow ups and initial meetings/calls with your identified prospects. (And I do recognise that Social Selling methods and tools also have both a valid and powerful place in the sales cycle today – but they can be measured too in this way too, if you use them). Next, if you are successful and gain a qualified prospect, you dive into the meat of the sales cycle – the exploration of their needs, meetings, demonstrations, presentations, negotiations and closing. The timings, order and 'weight' of each of these steps may differ (maybe your service or offering is never demonstrated, maybe it usually needs at least two demonstrations) but there will be recognised steps in your environment to move from a cold position to finally winning the business.

Perhaps you use one of the many available CRM systems. My contention is this. Both historically and today, paper-based and CRM systems seem to exist primarily to record the work done by individuals and to allow management to then analyse and compare performance. They also help sales managers to forecast the likely sales performance outcomes. I have some real issues with these systems in the way they frequently operate...

> 10 deals → $100K each → 30% likelihood rating each → = $300K 'likely to win' forecast?

Let's say you have 10 deals valued at $100K each in the pipeline at 30% likelihood of closing. Most CRM systems say you have $300K likely to close. WRONG! Currently you have no business likely to close. You have no deal at 50%+ chance of closing (BTW, forecasting likelihood and qualification is covered in chapter 12). Time and again I am asked by organisations to review forecasting as their forecast numbers never seem to be realised. This problem is, all too often, the core of the issue. Taking the total numbers in the pipeline (or even the deals in closing stage) and their individual percentage likelihood of closing, then extrapolating the gross 'possible' deal value number in the pipeline, divided by the percentage chance of winning each deal to arrive at a forecast is simply a false positive. But that's how the numbers seem to work in many organisations I meet (often called the weighted average forecasting approach). I disagree with both the premise and the calculation, and you need to be aware of this as you work to close deals and also discuss them with your manager. I don't want to seem critical, but I feel that a lot of CRM systems used today serve to record activity and then use logical calculation and accounting principles to weigh up their forecast likelihoods. However, it's the wrong mechanism being used in the wrong way, in the wrong place to achieve the end result you actually need.

However, far more important to my mind than the simple use of these numbers (however you do it and however it is measured) is the idea of the resulting 'conversion ratio' between your sales stages, which is not just the combination of any raw activity numbers being measured for their own sake. This was what I learned all those years ago – in those days it was recorded on a daily sheet of paper. But the recording mechanism doesn't concern me, it's the thought process that should be important to you.

Let's assume you have a target of $500K. Start with this end result in mind. Now look at your activity records. Then look at what they mean for you. Here's a simplified example. How many cold calls/social contacts/engagements does it take you to achieve one real conversation with a qualified new prospect? That's Ratio 1. How many of these identified prospects does it take you to get to the next stage – let's say a meeting to review their needs in detail or a demonstration of your solution? That's Ratio 2. How many demonstrations then lead to an agreement to quote (or explore needs or whatever is your next stage). That's Ratio 3. Perhaps finally you ask, how many of these quotation stage deals do you need to close one sale. That's Ratio 4. Now using simple arithmetic and your average deal size, you can very easily figure out (if your historic activity records in the CRM are reasonably accurate) how many cold calls a week or month YOU need to make to hit your annual target, how many demonstrations a month are needed, etc.

(Interestingly, the story I told in the previous chapter on Time Management featured a highly successful company early in my career. Their entire focus in 'CRM' terms (though they used pen and paper) was on those individual ratios.)

Here is a graphic highlighting a sample process (using a simplified example sales cycle with just 4 steps and ratios). In this scenario we have looked at our CRM data and have been able to establish the following facts about our own performance. In the last year, it took us 1,512 calls/social media contacts to get 126 meetings. It took three meetings to achieve one demo. Two demos were needed to get a formal quotation. Finally, it took three quotations to close one deal. If I now have a target of $500K and my average deal size is $80k then I can map out what I have to do each month or year to ensure we make target. You can also then use those ratios to define what you have to achieve at every step this month/year to ensure success...

With the real raw data from your CRM you can now map out how you will make your target. You are using the continuously recorded data to establish what YOU need to do to succeed on a monthly, quarterly or annual basis. It's based on those hard, historical facts and it lays out the level of work you must do at each pipeline stage in order to succeed. This, to my mind, is far more useful than just knowing how many cold calls you make, or how many deals are in your 'closing stage' (however it is defined) in isolation.

You also have the ability to look at how you are performing throughout the year at each ratio stage against your previous performance. This lets you spot trends and issues early and react to them. You can then map out what you have to do to succeed at each stage of your sales cycle, based on your own real experience and data. Everyone's numbers and ratios will be different, because we all have different skills and experience. Both paper systems and CRMs can provide you with the raw data to figure this out. With this knowledge you can then plan and execute for your own best results. And remember, you own your own data. Drag it back out of the system and use it to your own benefit. Think of this process as your own personal Business Intelligence output. It can give you the edge you need...

There is a simple ranking of the data that you use in any activity –

> Raw data → 2. Structured data → 3. Intelligence gleaned from that data → 4. Knowledge → 5. Wisdom

I believe that most sales people use the data they have to hand only at levels one and two without gaining real benefit from its existence. In fact, I accept that recording the data is a chore. Having real knowledge is the first goal – that is, properly understanding how you perform at each stage of the sales process. Then it's all about achieving wisdom – which is acting on that knowledge to improve your performance and optimise your work. What stages are roadblocks for you? Are individual ratios improving or getting worse? Why? Your CRM can help you to get there and as such it can be a really useful tool to help you to deliver the results you want and need. Knowing what you have to do to achieve the result you need at each stage of your sales cycle can be a powerful motivator and make an enormous difference to your performance.

And this philosophy doesn't just work for sales. If you are in a broader 'Business Development' role, then the same metrics can be applied to, for example, digital marketing. From click through to sale what are the ratios, where are the roadblocks and how can you improve?

If today, for whatever reason, you have no personal metrics, you have no control or management of your prospects and no direction. Get recording your activity and then extract all you can from the data you create – to your advantage. If the company doesn't do it, then start for your own benefit.

The Lesson
Put simply, don't just dump data into whatever system you have to use. Take that raw data and create your own measures – even if just on a sheet of handwritten paper – to work out how you perform and therefore what you need to do to achieve your goals. I know this sounds really simple, but in my experience far less that 10% of salespeople understand this and therefore know what they have to do, based on their own personal historic performance, in order to succeed.

To help you I have created a simple sample 1-page sheet that you can start to use or modify to suit your sales stages. Go to appendix 3 to view it or try it out...

"If we keep doing what we are doing, we're going to keep getting what we're getting..."

Stephen R Covey

Notes

Chapter 5
"Friends and Enemies - Political Selling"

"I can give you a six-word formula for success: Think things through - then follow through."

Edward Rickenbacker

Introduction

We all know that selling complex solutions and services into large, complex organisations is, well......... complex. Nothing is harder to master than dealing with the people you meet – at all levels. Political selling involves adding a layer of skills to traditional selling. This helps you stand out and map the target organisation better, where it matters most, in getting to the deal.

An Example

We are all familiar with the typical corporate organisation chart. It should exactly map the power lines in the structure. Who does what, who reports to whom? But, of course, there are always those who have little status but who do have real power. I was selling to a major manufacturing company and thought I understood everything well. But one name – of a front-line manager I had met only once – just kept on coming up on my radar. Eventually I couldn't resist, and I asked one of my main contacts (with whom I had established a good working relationship) who the person was. He smiled and then said *"I wondered if you would get there. He is a fairly junior manager, but he's also a close relative of the CFO! While he has no real role in what you are doing you can bet he is sharing his thoughts on the suppliers he has met and what his team think."* And there it was, a striking example of this issue. Someone who you might be tempted to ignore or dismiss, but who had more real influence than most executives – and the CFO was the ultimate decision maker here. As you might imagine, my planning and activities then altered substantially to ensure he was included and considered in everything we then did. But, how often do we unconsciously bypass these people and miss out on their support or at least tacit approval?

So, there are, in reality, two organisations. First the traditional, formal structure. And second, the true power and influence lines - and I would argue it's those that you need to try and identify as a priority. Of course, they may coincide but how often have you heard of a techie or specialist being talked of in hushed tones? I bet there is at least one in your own organisation. Maybe with no real formal position or status, but their knowledge and skills make them a critical person to target – if you can find them from the outside. Asking some simple questions can often lead you to the hidden power brokers. *"Is there anyone in the organisation that is always consulted on technical issues? Is there a technical or financial specialist that's always involved in this sort of decision? Do you have a person, like we do, that is always asked to review potential suppliers and buying decisions?"* And that leads me on to the next consideration –

Most traditional sales skills training manuals talk about getting to the most senior person you can, ideally the final decision maker. That is good and right. You want to influence and sell at the highest level. But, in my experience, those very people are also the most sophisticated and capable at handling sales people – they tell them what they want to hear, they exaggerate or underestimate a situation or cost, they can play 'Sales Poker'. I find that as you try to head ever further upwards it is a great investment to also nurture someone well below the upper echelons of decision making. They will typically be more open once the relationship is established, and they sometimes, in my experience, tend to enjoy and share 'the gossip' more. Most importantly, you can ask them the big questions that relate to your chances without impacting the higher-level executives impression of you. *"Tell me, is the organisation typically making leading edge investments or is it a bit more conservative?"* *"I know that Yvonne is the main decision maker – who has her ear these days?"* *"If you were me, is there anyone else that you would have spoken to?"* I am sure you can think of other test questions you would love to ask at the higher level but are a bit concerned about asking directly. You are, of course, building a relationship and trust with all these contacts as you go along...

But what if you suspect not everyone is being honest and up front? Perhaps they favour another vendor, or they dislike you or your company for some historic reason? It's hard to find out, isn't it? In the next chapter I will go into detail on some ways to manage that. Suffice it to say now, that laying out a few leading statements to the most likely 'suspects' – different facts or information for each – can let you see who is not on side by the responses that then come back from them and/or their colleagues as they feed their personal prejudices into the process.

Your own team can help you enormously. One of the best run sales organisations I have worked for had a 'teams of two' approach to sales. Every sales person had a directly partnered technical pre-sales person working with them alone. More than that, the pre-sales head earned a subset of the sales persons commission plan too. This is, of course, very expensive to achieve, but... Now you had a truly joined up team, both focussed on exactly the same objective. And here's the payback. Once a sales campaign had started in a target account, the pre-sales head would go in (always on their own) to meet with their technical peers and while chatting they would ask all these political and positioning questions. Their contacts ALWAYS gave them far more information than was shared with the salesperson – *"We know they are only interested in the money".* These pre-sales heads became phenomenal resources, they were trusted technical advisors who could ask questions, establish the real needs and increase customer confidence in the vendor. It's no coincidence that many of the most successful companies, certainly in IT, use variants of this approach to really find out exactly what is going on and what the reality of the situation is. Who do you have available that could perform that role? As well as pre-sales, I have seen technical specialists, customer service managers and support staff, finance directors, and executives used to meet their peers and increase the chances of gaining a win.

Finally, talking about using your own senior managers and executives, there are a few points to make here. If you bring in an executive to 'mirror' their peer in the prospect organisation, make sure they are at the right level. You must ensure that they really are peers. Taking your Board level person in to meet a mid-level manager sends all the wrong messages. And if you are using an executive, take (or even force) the time to brief them properly. This can be a bit intimidating the first time you do it. Tell them what the situation is. Why you want them to come in with you. Give them a pen picture of who they will be meeting.

AND finally, agree and set their goals for the meeting. I have done this a lot of times as the salesperson, then later in my career I became the executive being ushered in. Trust me in this, any good executive would far rather hear from a salesperson that is running and directing the campaign as though it is their own business and who has planned what needs to be achieved than a soft *"Well, just do what you think is right"* approach. Be assertive and clear in what you want from them. Be specific on the commitments and answers you need. In my experience any good executive will relish the challenge – and many can't wait to tell you how well they have done when they come back out! On the other hand, weak executives are clearly uncomfortable in anything other than a hand shaking exercise – don't use them again if at all possible. It's your account, your campaign, your business.

My most extreme memory of this? I had three executives set for critical morning meetings in a world-famous prospective client. All had flown in the previous day from various countries. We met up in the hotel bar mid evening and I (with no little nervousness may I say) told them there would be no dinner until we had gone through everything for the meetings the next day and agreed what role each had and their personal objectives. There was silence for a couple of seconds, then the most senior executive (a full five tiers further up the organisation to me) said *"And quite right too, we're not here to party, we are here to help – let's start"*...

The Lesson
Don't just do the basics. Dig into the dynamics of the target organisation and work your contacts, both at the highest level possible and also lower down at the same time. Aim to manage the normal process but also find and work with the power brokers and experts that lie inside the prospect. Then gain leverage by using your specialists and executives at the right time for maximum impact.

> *"It's during collaboration [between buyers & sellers] that ideas are born and insights come alive."*
> **Erica Stritch**

Notes

Chapter 6

The B2B Switch Sell

"A smooth sea never made a skilled sailor..."

Anon

Introduction
The idea of switch selling has a very negative connotation in general usage. You think you are getting something but then end up with something inferior. But what if the switch was seriously - and definitely - to both the vendor and their customer's advantage – big time? How would you feel as a customer then? In the very biggest, and most complex deals, there are many factors at play. In these situations, internal politics and vendor favouritism can come into play with a vengeance. A lot of the people you meet could be 'players' who might be looking to achieve something for themselves and/or to manipulate the process towards their favoured vendor. This is neither 'bad' nor 'good', it is just human nature playing out within a corporate organisation. But when you are trying to unseat a powerful incumbent in one of their own most favoured accounts is there something you can do to take advantage of this human behaviour? Oh yes...

An Example
First, let me say that while this example may be about some of the world's most powerful computers of their time, the principle works equally well with any big-ticket hardware or software ranges, or families of capital goods, or professional services, or printing presses, or car fleets, or planes, or consulting programmes, or large-scale support contracts, or enterprise-wide business projects. Let me also say that this particular technique only works where product or service 'ranges' or offerings compete and can be compared to each other. This is a very specific technique that you might be able to use perhaps only once or twice in your career, but it can be truly devastating to the competition. Where there is only a single, hard-defined, point solution from you and each of the competitors this approach doesn't work – as you will see from the story that follows...

A pre-sales colleague and I were selling into a major international organisation based on the East Coast of the

USA. To give some context, our whole local operation totalled just four heads. Our competitor (and in the end it was a two-way fight) was the incumbent. They had a very large local operation, including a six-eight head team on site within the target organisation. They had been the strategic supplier to the customer for many years. Working relationships existed between senior staff and executives at all levels. They were the de facto industry leader in this market segment and had some superb technology – as had we. The prospect had increased their IT workloads and decided it was time to massively upgrade their computing power. Everyone was very welcoming to us and open as we discussed their needs and our capabilities. As we worked through the selection process, over about five months, we started to realise that things we said to some of their staff were being queried and played back – with our competitor's counter messaging – quite frequently. We realised that it was perhaps possible that one or more contacts were gathering data from us for the competitor to respond to and act against.

Working with my Sales Leader and the Country CEO (who were both fantastic tacticians) we decided on a plan to turn this to our advantage. We were going to use the 'judo principle' – taking our competitors strength and leverage and turning it back on them. It was a principle I understood well, having reached the highest possible level in judo myself as a 'junior' many years previously.

So how did it work? Both vendors had a range of technology that the customer could use. The customer's needs were starting to get quite close to the top of both supplier's ranges. We went in, analysed their needs in a lot of detail and then aggressively positioned our second top offering - a very, very powerful computer system. It was exactly the right size solution and a highly logical fit. We sold the technology, we sold its capability, we fought directly with our competitor for month after month using industry data and claim - v – their counter claim on our relative performance to their equivalent second top offering. The fight was long and hard and culminated in reference visits organised by both competitors to various end user organisations that had installed these competing technologies. We were asked for indicative pricing by some of the staff and provided it openly and accurately.

We put in our substantial and highly detailed proposal and it was well received. We also agreed that any detail changes would be communicated before they made their final decision. A day was set for their executive committee to meet and decide which vendor to go with. Half an hour before the meeting I delivered a personal letter to their CTO explaining that we had decided that, with everything else being equal and unchanged, we would be delivering our largest system, not the second largest, if they decided to go with us. This had been our plan all along. By positioning the second highest offering in our range, our competitor had both priced and reacted technically against it. They had detailed how their equivalent technology was, quite correctly – and ever so marginally – more powerful than our offering and their internal friends had maybe helped to reinforce that message. But in doing so they had also unwittingly agreed, positioned and confirmed that this also meant that our largest system was MUCH more powerful than their second top offering.

They had positioned themselves into a losing situation, primarily through their own use of 'intelligence' and that potential internal help. And, guess what, their pricing was almost identical to ours for their second largest offering! Oh, and another thing, our two site visits to our reference customers were both to large organisations that just 'happened to have' two of our systems – the second largest and the largest, so our existing customers had already talked about the real-world performance of both with the prospect. The decision came immediately in our favour and despite intense 'after the fact' politicking it remained our deal. Their whole account was lost to them and we took over.

We had delivered a solution which really exceeded the customer's expectations. They were ecstatic. They received more than they expected. We got the deal we had always planned to get. We were more than happy. Our competitor was the only one who lost out – truly a <u>positive</u> switch sell... ☺

A little postscript. Many years later I changed jobs to a new industry sector. At a business meeting I was introduced to an individual who it turned out had then been a Senior Executive at the competitive vendor during the time of the deal discussed above – we had both since moved to other employers and sectors. As we chatted, I decided to tell him I was the salesman who had won that deal all those years ago and taken the account off them. He stared at me for a second, glowered a bit, then burst out laughing... *"What a fabulous deal, you totally screwed us that day"*.

The Lesson
Even when everything is stacked against you there are ways, with careful planning and execution, to manage things towards your favour. Assuming of course that you do have a valid solution to the problem. If you don't, then all of the above doesn't work. Looking at the strategy, perhaps you can see how the same approach would work in offering a range of services, consulting projects or capital goods or software. But this is a one-off tactic. You couldn't use it against any competent rival anytime soon after, or in the same geography for a very long time, but as a one-time tactic for that very, very big deal against the odds, it is unbeatable.

"Buyers want to be surprised and inspired."

Rain Group

Notes

Chapter 7

Ask the Dumb Questions

"The greatest gift is not being afraid to question."

Ruby Dee

Introduction
Who doesn't admire good old Columbo? That famous TV detective with the rumpled coat who seems to be laughed at in every episode, until, just as he is being thrown out by the oh, so smug villain (who has definitely got off with the crime) turns and says *"Oh, just one more thing..."* Out comes the question and it's all over again for another episode! Now, his final question is always clever, incisive and powerful. But sometimes the 'dumb' question has a lot of power too...

An Example
In this case I can think of three instances where this principle was proven to me. In the earliest example I wasn't trying to be clever, I really did just ask the dumb question... ☺

I was selling into a well-known and conservatively run government body. The technology I was working with was usually leased to the customer by the vendor or a financial intermediary. I was sitting with a mid-level technical Manager and trying to figure out if I had a path to a sale or whether I should just qualify out and move onto another prospect. It was very marginal. I heard myself say *"If the current equipment is all leased can you arrange for me to see the details of the leases?"* The individual thought for a second then said *"No one has ever asked for that before, but if it might help to get a better result for us, why not..."* Not quite believing what had just happened, I was taken along a corridor into the small office of a cost accountant buried in the depths of their very old and beautiful building – who had probably never before seen a salesperson in their domain. The manager explained who I was and asked her to give me the information I needed, then he left. A chair was found, and I sat beside her. She was helpful and kept great records! Two minutes later I was looking at the full lease history, timescales, end dates, monthly payments, residual values and capital costs for all the incumbent supplier's installed solutions. They would have had kittens had they known what I was being shown. I was gifted a print out of the information and left, dazed but very happy. About three weeks later I was the proud owner of a very nice Purchase Order – my quote just happened to be exactly the right price, to be installed at the very best time, with a 'just lower' monthly cost than they currently paid and a nice end of current lease payout for the government body that had to show 'best value' to its citizens – spooky eh?

On another occasion I sat beside an IT manager in one of Europe's biggest insurance companies. She was 'switched on' and more than able to say no to requests from salespeople. We were getting along reasonably well so I explained that at a personal level I was really struggling to visualise the enormous IT Department (several hundred heads in multiple groups and sub groups) and did she know of a way to help me? After a few seconds she said, *"Well I guess I could give you an organisation chart."* I agreed that would be very helpful and she keyed in a few entries then her desktop printer started up. This was in the days of the 'fan-fold' paper, dot matrix printers. The printer went at it for about 5-6 minutes then she handed me the large printout stack. I was a bit confused but just said thanks. After the session finished, I went back to my office and started unfolding the report. It wasn't a standard 'external view' high-level organisation chart, it was their internal working organisational document with every person in the organisation, their title and role, current project responsibilities, their reporting line, email address and direct phone number – over 20 pages worth!

It's also worth mentioning that as you engage with a new prospect, or take over an existing account, there is a 'golden period' for the first 30-60 days when you are truly entitled to ask as many 'dumb' questions as you can. People will usually forgive you because you *"Don't know the background and all the history".* Use that time and those questions wisely...

Don't ever be concerned about saying *"I'm sorry but I don't know".* Salespeople frequently seem to need to answer every question immediately – even if they don't actually know the right answer. Say you don't know and then DO get back to them – this is a great technique to prove you are both human and conscientious. And it also allows for another communication later, above and beyond what is already committed.

Finally, I was lucky enough to hear a great speaker – an individual who has been described as the world's greatest negotiator – Herb Cohen. (Look him up on Google or YouTube, I can't recommend him highly enough). In the midst of his highly entertaining hour of advice, experience, laughs and education he said, *"Do you know what the best questions to ask are to get more information?"* They are *"eh?"* and *"Huh?"* And he is right. No matter the situation, just say one of these 'words' – and then shut up – and the other party will try to explain better and give you more information than they already have.

The Lesson
Sometimes we are frightened to ask a question. Will we look stupid? Is it too much? What if the answer is negative? But, if we don't ask, how can we move towards the right answer for the customer, alter direction, then do what's right? In selling, and in life, those 'dumb' questions aren't so dumb after all...

"The smart ones ask when they don't know. And sometimes when they do."

Malcolm Forbes

Notes

Chapter 8
Really Understand the Target Organisation

"Knowledge is power? No. Knowledge on its own is nothing, but the application of useful knowledge, now that is powerful."

Rob Liano

Introduction
If you are reading this book – and have made it this far (congratulations, give yourself a pat on the back ☺) then you are seriously interested in B2B/Enterprise Selling. I am guessing you might even have had some sales training; you know the sales process; you understand the need to have multiple contacts in the account you are either defending or targeting. But what else could you do to make a positive impact?

An Example
I once met an individual who had become very successful in their chosen field. It wasn't a world I would ever relish selling into. This older gentleman (and he really was older, as I now am - on reflection) sold electrical, plumbing and mechanical parts into ironmongers and small, high street DIY stores. You know them, those wonderful old shops where they can find anything you want. *"The outlet pipe on my 25-year-old Electrolux washing machine has split, can you help?"* They reply, *"Wait there, I am sure I have one of those somewhere".* And off they wander, coming back in a minute or two with exactly what you need. (For those readers not from the UK, can I suggest that for some light relief you look up 'The Two Ronnies – Fork Handles' – set in one of these shops and possibly the best piece of wordplay comedy ever written – and still, after 40 years, the UK's best loved comedy sketch of all time)

Every day this person drove around a wide geographic area, dropping into those shops asking if they needed anything he could supply. I could only imagine how soul destroying and mind numbing this would be – *"no"* after *"no"* after *"no"* after *"no".* But he had somehow become really successful and enjoyed his work! What had he done? He explained that he had looked at the job in what we would today describe as 'holistic' terms. He decided to 'live' in their world. He subscribed to their trade journals, he researched new tools and devices that they could sell, he read about trends in the High Street. Then, when he dropped in, he chatted about their lives, their world, their issues.

Soon his large customer base each looked forward to him dropping in and sharing some conversation – and they almost all found things he could supply on each visit to make it 'worth his while' to return soon. At the same time, he saw his rivals being turned away every day... What had he done? He had changed from 'just another salesman' to someone who knew their issues, goals and challenges. And for many, he became a friend. Not an acquaintance when it suited, but a real friend. How did all those other 'door to door' reps do when they competed with him? It's not hard to guess, is it? Even if their 'goods' were a percent or two cheaper in that commodity world. If it was you that ran the shop, would you give away that knowledge, market place expertise, useful hints and relationship just for 2% off a single transaction – of course you wouldn't.

At the start of my career I wanted to find out more about the biggest local bank to help me sell into them. I had to use a typewriter (!) to type a letter to post by snail mail to their Company Secretary asking for any recent statements or annual reports they might agree to send me. After about ten days I received a few items that helped – a bit. Now compare that to today. If I put the name of that UK bank into any search engine how many results would there be? If I put in 'press releases' how many articles would be available? If I said 'strategy' what would the results look like? Well, for the sake of research, I have just done exactly that right now, and the answers are, in the same order – 76.6 million, 125 million and 13.5 million!

Today we are truly blessed when compared to every previous generation. Those distractions I talked about in the fourth chapter can also be a massive aid to our sales planning and execution. You have more background information available than you could ever read, never mind use. Now, Social Selling has a very strong place in today's business mix. But do we make our first social contact, or physically go in and in either case just talk about our product/service or their lives, concerns and goals? Every organisation you sell to – either formally or informally – has their own 'Project New Start', 'The 5 goals for FY20', 'The 3-year Strategy' etc. Even a small organisation will know what 'the boss' wants this year. I bet your own organisation has its own internal targets and strategies...

So, you need to make effective use of the best information that is available. If you are going in for a meeting, quickly look at what has come up in the last month or so online. Check for anything about their successes or failures, their path to meeting their goals (if they are struggling to make their goals and the markets are commentating, or if they are 'flying', at least now you know in which way to position your offerings, and what their underlying internal mood will be like). The list of what's available today is for practical usage, unlimited. What do I focus on myself? –

- Annual and quarterly reports. Particularly the summary and CEO and Chairman statements.

- Recent press releases

- Recent press coverage – bad and good

- Reports or articles on their marketplace and its dynamics

- Google Alerts enable you to receive updates on information you want, proactively, at intervals that work for you – a useful tool

- Some of the above on their competitors

- And of course, Linkedin is a really useful tool too

With this information you can truly differentiate from the competition. Show that you know their world, their industry, their goals and challenges. If you were them would you listen to a product salesman or someone who had prepared in this way?

The Lesson
Think of that humble, quiet, sales superstar I described above. Follow his example in your own way and in your own world and you too will succeed.

"You can make more friends in two months by becoming interested in other people than you can in two years by trying to get other people interested in you."

Dale Carnegie

Notes

Chapter 9

Don't Forget the Board (and Others)

"Judgement comes from experience and great judgement comes from bad experience."

Bob Packwood

Introduction
This is the shortest chapter of the book, but the lesson is really important. It is all about looking beyond the expected and typical decision makers...

An Example
I had conducted what I believed to be a really strong campaign into a very large organisation based in mainland Europe. And when I say large, I mean humungous. I was pleased that I had managed to get all the way to the influencers and decision makers. I had checked that I had the right people 'ticked off'. They had all bought in. They proactively asked me for a proposal and quote and I then met the final – and very senior - decision maker to go over everything. He was happy with the proposal. He confirmed that they would go ahead, he had the authority. I asked what the actual physical order process was, and he explained that all capital purchases over a (very, very high) amount were signed off by the Executive Board. However, not once in his long career had they ever turned back a request or changed it, the Board acted only in a supervisory way and didn't interfere with operational budgets and decisions.

About five days later he called and told me to stand by as the Executive Board was meeting that afternoon and he would be sending through the order paperwork, which was already prepared, in about an hour. I sat in my office until after 8pm then went home, puzzled and worried.

At 9am the next day I called him. When his secretary put me through, I knew instantly that something was badly wrong. The senior executive was genuinely upset and embarrassed. Not only had the Board rejected the decision but they had decided to sign up with our rival supplier. I couldn't speak for a few moments, and his unhappiness also washed over the call. I asked several times *"why?"* and *"how?"* and he then told me something I didn't know – because I hadn't ever asked. One of the external and

Non-Executive Directors on the Board happened to be the European CEO of one of our rivals. *"But Non-Execs aren't allowed to comment or interfere when the matter is in their own area of business"* he explained. But something had happened somehow, the deal was done. Another salesperson had done to me, what I enjoyed doing to others. They had figured out a way to close me out without my knowledge. We never did find out what was maybe said, done, suggested, threatened, hinted or advised in that room but it was probably the worst day of my selling career (and yes, I had already told my boss and his boss that we had the deal – you can imagine the phone calls I had to make). Someone outside of the company decision process and also outside the lines of authority had possibly done something to alter a done deal. If they hadn't it was a pretty weird coincidence! It was one of the worst but most powerful lessons of my career. I will likely go to my grave not knowing what was done – but the lesson was learnt.

Both experienced and inexperienced (me included, as you have just read) salespeople can decide the deal is theirs BEFORE they have the contract signed and sealed. We are all optimists. Never, ever, ever, do this. No matter what the internal pressure is, only say *"It's looking good"* or similar internally until it's done and immovable.

The Lesson
So today, when in a similar position (or advising those who are) I not only cover the usual thinking about decision makers and influencers, I also look upward and outward to external Directors and advisors and anyone else who might be able to do or say something beyond the formal structure – where are they from, what is their agenda, how would they view a decision in our favour? This principle is so important it's worth two quotes...

"Many a slip twixt the cup and the lip."
Shakespeare

"We learn from failure, not from success!"
Bram Stoker

Notes

Chapter

10

Keep the Competition Busy

"If he sends reinforcements everywhere, he will everywhere be weak. Thus, the expert in battle moves the enemy, and is not moved by him."

Sun Tzu

Introduction
Every organisation, no matter how large, has limited resources to bring to bear on any given situation. Other internal priorities serve to remove resources and reduce capability. This is a fact of life that you can use to heavily impact your competitors, especially when you are the smaller player in a sector or geography.

An Example
A good friend of mine, running a small satellite sales office against larger competitors in a large conurbation told a story where he likened his team to that famous scene we have all watched in the traditional 'Cowboys and Indians' movies of old. The heroes are desperate and surrounded, their enemy massively outnumbers them and has all the advantages. All is lost. Suddenly a cloud of dust can be seen in the distance. It is enormous and moving fast – it has to be at least two to three hundred relief soldiers or warriors arriving! The attackers flee and soon after, only two or three riders arrive, each pulling a large brush behind their horses.

What on earth does that have to do with B2B/Enterprise Selling? Well, in this example there was a perception of power, capability to execute and activity that spooked those attackers. Therein lies the message. If your competitor is trying to respond to actions you have taken, even if not real or serious, they will be less able, focussed and resourced to deal with your actual campaign – which you can run quietly and less disturbed by them.

How do you achieve this condition? There are several tactics that I have used successfully over the years –

1. Look at the campaign you want to run for real. Then sit and think for a while about what else would worry the competition. Create a second, perhaps much more visible campaign with an offer, a special deal, a trial, a concept that will worry them. Launch it loud and broadly. If it serves to disturb them and demands a response, good. If you actually get a lead from it, so much the better. Either way it's a win/win for you. (that's a phrase coined in the 1960's by Herb Cohen from chapter 7)

2. Within a target account and once you are actively engaged... Look for everything you can influence or suggest. Keep your own focus on your internally stated goal but open up as many other lines of attack as you can – a strong competitor will want to respond to them all to block you off. Losing or not moving forward on the others will not impact you, but it will impact the competitor. And again, there is always the chance of unexpected upside. I have won deals that have pivoted to one of these diversionary 'rockets' that I had launched, instead of my original plan!

3. Think about what you are really good at, your strongest 'unique'. Can you sell it with relatively little effort or resource? Then hit all your competitor's accounts with messaging about that solution/offer/idea. If it is your strongest point they will struggle, in every account, to respond effectively and they will be pressured everywhere. They will want to protect what is theirs already. You can suck up all that comes from this attack, in the knowledge that your competition will be struggling and expending energy. At the same time, then go on to sell another of your 'strategic' or 'alternative' offerings into the accounts you have already chosen to target. While the competition is engaged defensively, they will likely not even know about your other focused activity...

The Lesson
In your sector or geography, try to achieve three things. First play to your strengths. Second, ensure the competition is never sure what you are doing. Third, aim to stretch competitive resources as much as you can. Keep your focus, work to reduce theirs. With distraction comes opportunity...

"The whole secret lies in confusing the enemy, so that he cannot fathom our real intent."

Sun Tzu

Notes

Chapter 11

Care, But Not That Much

"Unless we learn to know ourselves, we run the danger of destroying ourselves."

Ja Jahannes

Introduction

The title of this chapter is a variant of a statement made by Herb Cohen. When I heard him say it, I found it aptly described an attitude that we need to have in our selling lives and which I felt I already understood implicitly. In fact, it is often critical to success. I had already understood this principle – without such a succinct description - from the very beginning of my career and have seen its impact many times...

An Example

As sales people we are goaled and motivated to 'need' to win every deal. We are positive and enthusiastic, and we are also keen, sometimes desperate, to win. It may be counter intuitive but that very attitude can either make us lose the deal or reduce our negotiating strength. What's the problem? Put simply, I have frequently wanted a deal 'too much'. Some examples...

Let me start with one situation where I was in a meeting with a colleague who proved the concept by doing the exact opposite. We were visiting a very hard-nosed buyer who started the meeting by disparaging our product and pricing (to support his plan to get a big discount I presume). We were in big ticket territory. My colleague was, however, over goal and also in the process of moving to another role in the company a long distance away from our office (unknown to the buyer). *"Well, I understand your position and your choice and accept that we can't do anything for you, so thanks for your time"* he said. It wasn't stated as a tactic or technique, he was actually interested in doing business, but not to the point of desperation. He really genuinely did get up and closed his briefcase, moving towards the door. *"Stop"* came the shout from the buyer, *"I am interested..."*. Just how far had the power dynamic moved in that few seconds? Shortly after, we concluded a deal with the buyer.

Later in my career I was running a business operation for

a large multi-national. German owned, with the normal pressures to deliver results, we were more than a little keen to ensure each quarter was a success. But in being so keen we had pretty well gifted marketplace control to our end customers. The product was a value-added technology of reasonable value. On reviewing our quarterly performance, I realised that up to 70% of the business done was concluded in the last 72 hours of the quarter and the discounts were way over target during that period. We were being just too keen to sell, and sophisticated buyers then waited until the maximum point of leverage before starting to negotiate. Having decided to take action, it took a massive effort across the organisation, combined with a large number of angry conversations with upset procurement officers who were used to 'the game' before our customer friends found out that the price wasn't going to continue to go down at the end of every quarter.

After the drama of our change in direction and the refusal to drop the prices for a couple of quarter ends, magically, discounts overall then reduced and the end of quarter pressure on our manufacturing operation massively dropped too. The end-user customers got their systems quicker (and when they needed them, not when their procurement people said they could buy) and were happier with the more stable business partnership so it was actually, once again, a win/win for both parties.

Have you found yourself giving off 'desperation vibes' as a deal slips or the competition seem to have the edge? I know that I have – it's human nature. But, when you say *"I need it, I am really desperate to get this particular deal"* in what direction is the balance of power moving? Away from you every time...

This is one of the hardest attributes to learn. Even if you don't say any words your frequency of communication and body language can shout *"I'm desperate"* to the other party.

I am lucky, I can now look back over a long career. In counting I found that I had survived and prospered over 120 consecutive quarters before I left the corporate world to start out on my own! But guess what, while they each seemed so critical in the moment, can I remember more than a handful of quarter ends? No. Can I remember the individual deals that I was freaked out about? No. Do I remember the details of those situations, good or bad? No. Can I visualize the day and time the good or bad news came? No! I can truly say that those individual deals and quarters did matter, but not really too much. I know it is easy for me to say, but having the attitude that you do care, but it's not that critical, will give you the positioning to be more successful.

The Lesson
Selling is infectious. We crave success. But stepping back just a little can actually increase your chances. You still need hard work, skill and initiative, but beware those vibes that tell the other party you are overly keen and, over time, your results will be stronger!

"Who you are is speaking so loudly that I can't hear what you're saying."

Ralph Waldo Emerson

Notes

Chapter 12

Qualification

"Avoid selling to dumb customers, there aren't enough left!"

Jasleen Gumber

Introduction
In every sales school, class, academy, 'How to' book and presentation, the subject of Qualification always comes up. It does so for a very simple reason. Qualification is one of the most basic, but also most essential skills for all sales people to learn and then use. But, as I mentioned in chapter 3, salespeople are creative and hate forms and process. I do too. Qualification is an important exception for me, doing something process-based here is liable to repay you a hundred-fold. It's worth the pain...

An Example
This subject is so broad and ingrained that there is no single example that stands out for me. In this section I will therefore discuss the 'why' and some of the best tools I am aware of – regardless of your market or your solutions portfolio.

We are all busy. We are mostly over-committed. Our pipeline needs filling. We have to close transactions as fast as possible. We are also scared to drop those deals we have in our pipeline as we have already invested the effort and they may pay off, right? This is the issue. We can either spend our time going further and further down the rat hole with every deal that appears, or become much more focussed and selective. In my consulting work I have visited a very large number of sales teams. I have yet to see a scatter gun approach anywhere, yield the same results as real focus, combined with serious qualification.

Now, many salespeople say to me *"Of course I qualify, I do it all the time. I don't need a process or form to help me"*. They are plain wrong.

Proper qualification needs you to consider all the factors at play. I have been on countless visits with good – and great – salespeople but have never met anyone who can remember to query every possible factor or area that could impact the deal. There are just too many. That's where a simple process, in support of your creativity, skills and experience, is invaluable.

This chapter is not a sales pitch for one of the available qualification tools against another. I really want to raise awareness and to have you actively seek out yourself the one that fits you best. And boy, is there a choice available! Stepping back a lot of years for a moment –

It was away back in the mists of the end of the 1970's/early 1980's and I was sent on a training course by my employer. The trainer was running a detailed course on selling. But the section that caught my interest was the 1-page qualification tool – 'SCOTSMAN' – a mnemonic for the eight areas he believed you had to review and measure to increase your chances of success. It was simple, fast and elegant. And it helped me! Fast forward ten years and I was starting work with another vendor. They had also adopted SCOTSMAN but theirs had been adapted in conjunction with the trainer to precisely fit their needs. I still have both these original sheets today. This tool has since been very widely adopted and adapted world-wide. It is used – and customised – across lots of industries. Looking on Google today I found over 130,000 articles and images with individual variations of the original single page concept.

Widening the Google search to the more general 'Sales qualification tools' today yields 45.5 million hits. Titles like BANT (an even simpler tool, credited I believe to IBM in the first instance), TAS Qualification, ADOPTED, CUTE, MEDDIC and CHAMP pop up, along with many others. Each has its own strengths and uses. The point is this. Whichever of these mechanisms you review, analyse and then adopt, having a single way to measure likelihood (so what exactly does 80% likely to close mean to you, to your colleagues, to your manager? How do you define it?) and to look at the gaps in your knowledge so you can qualify better – or out – will always improve your deal closing percentage. It will also lead you to focus on the deals that are actually winnable and help you see past the natural optimism of the salesperson! I cannot emphasise the importance of professional and logical qualification enough.

Not only does the use of a qualification tool help you win more business, deal by deal, but you will also be able to more easily spot the areas where you tend to stall or lose. You can then consider your skills and approach and develop and focus your efforts to improve into those 'problem' areas.

Oh, and by the way, if you have lost two or three deals in a row that you rated at 90% you are definitely qualifying and measuring your pipeline incorrectly. Any deal at 90% should always come in, unless you are being careless or untruthful to yourself (excluding my own lost deal in chapter 9 of course ☺). I often come across this exact malaise. Lots of deals at very high percentage likelihood. But very few deals closing. It just simply isn't right. Every time you take a deal to 80 or 90%+ it should be a genuine physical shock if it doesn't come in – and a once a year anomaly at worst. Be honest with yourself, think about what you do know, the gaps, the known unknowns (as per Donald Rumsfelt – the things you know you don't know) and those unknown unknowns (what else don't you know or haven't considered that could happen along the way to derail your campaign).

The Lesson
This one is easy – and proven all around the world and across every industry, profession and sector. Go beyond gut feel and apply some science to your prospective deals and their chance of closing. Is it worth continuing? What do you still need to find out? Is it actually a good deal for your company? Can you win it? Let the experience of the millions of salespeople around the world who have already looked at qualification and adopted a tool, help and guide you – research those sales qualification tools and then just do it...

"Big things are accomplished through the perfection of minor details."

John Wooden

Notes

Chapter

13

What is Real Value?

*"Price is what you pay.
Value is what you get..."*

Warren Buffett

Introduction

There are two core measures of value. The first is about beliefs and the core principles of an organisation (*"Our values"*). But value is also the principle that defines why we ever manage to sell anything to an organisation. In the corporate world, organisations don't usually buy because they see something they fancy. They buy to deal with, control, improve or better manage an element of their business.

An Example

There are, of course, business school definitions of this version of value. My MBA classes covered this issue along with all the other critical business measures. In addition, there are multiple discussions and definitions about business value on-line. Put very simply, value could, for example, be defined as –

Value = The benefit delivered, minus the total cost to deliver it. So, $V = (B-C)$. Alternatively, Webster's Dictionary says value in business is *"The monetary worth of something - market price. Or a fair return or equivalent in goods, services, or money for something exchanged."*

What does all this mean? As Warren Buffett so aptly and simply puts it above, as the customer you pay a price so you can then receive the value. Of course, Procurement departments always want to commoditise the products, services and solutions from vendors so that the cost is the only item being measured. Sales professionals must fight against this all the way. Think of it this way. If you sell something at a total cost to the customer of $100K, that then delivers a real value of $700K back to the buyer, is that really a worse deal for them than their spending only $50K up front (well done procurement, you won!) but then achieving just $80K value in return? Of course not, it is that delta – the value - between the two that is the most important measure in the real world. The end user needs, indeed craves, the value you can deliver to them. At every stage of the sales cycle you must look to establish how much value and benefit will be delivered – so that can be weighed against their investment.

Value thinking. A principle was once explained to me that helps in this endeavour. Let's say you are selling competitively to a large corporation. There is effectively a hierarchy of selling approaches –

1. I have a product that is really good

2. I have a product that can help you – here are the benefits it delivers

3. I can work with you to help you make your customers become more successful – and drive your competitive position

4. On the same basis as 3, I can work with you to help your customer's customers become more successful

In other words, you can sell a product to them. Or, you could sell a product with some specified benefits to them. Or, you could sell a solution that helps them to deliver more value to their own customers. Or, ultimately, you could position yourself as selling a solution that helps their customer's customers succeed.

Now reverse that for a moment to see how strong this approach is. You are the buyer. Three vendors are competing to sell you a product or service of some sort. But one other vendor is suggesting that they can help your company to better sell into your target market, so much so that your sales force can claim to be able to deliver more value directly to their clients, and that the clients in turn can add more value to their customers. Suddenly one vendor is talking about your entire business ecosystem and helping you to gain market share and revenues. Which one of the four would intrigue you? Which would likely have higher level conversations with you? I appreciate that, depending on the market, this could be a stretch. But certainly, step three, helping your prospect to deliver more value to their own customers (or reducing their costs so they can be more cost effective in what they do for their customers) should always be achievable. You are no longer pushing a product or service; you are talking about their need to increase their business value. An underpinning phrase I always remember from my first training course way back in the 1970's to help you define the benefit received is *"Which means that". "Our Acme 1000 generates widgets 20% faster... which means that...". "Our consulting services will enable you to gain market share in the manufacturing sector market, which means that..."*. You are now starting to define the benefit that will be derived, not the product. Extending this 'reach' as far down the prospects own value chain as possible will help you to differentiate yourself to them.

Some try to prove a form of value through customer satisfaction. That's better than nothing. But far better, as Sequent always espoused, is to aim for customer success. After all, who ever saw a customer whose partnership with you ended in great success being unsatisfied? And conversely, when what you deliver is unsuccessful how can there ever be customer satisfaction? Customer satisfaction is just the measure achieved from customer success or the lack of it – so the aim must be to deliver success - first and foremost.

I have only twice seen this value approach taken to the absolute extreme in sales terms. Perhaps even 'way over the top' – but the basic concept behind these actions could be very useful to you. I worked for a short time inside a large capital goods sales organisation in the USA and then later a smaller organisation in Northern mainland Europe. In each of these cases one individual had taken things right to the very edge in this regard. Only two people in my entire career! They had both separately and individually adopted the same, very interesting (but really aggressive) approach. On every deal, small or large, transactional or strategic, they made notes on the solution and what value they had committed to deliver and then ALWAYS called the customer back after some time had passed to confirm the specifics of the value that was actually delivered. *"We reduced days to manufacture by x". "We took one person out of the cost to build". "We speeded up our administration process by 10%"* etc. One returned quickly to the customer to remind them of what value they had received and to push for more add-on business there and then. The other used that knowledge when getting to the end of their fiscal year and trying to make the last deals to achieve their target. The individual called those customers again and the conversations went like this... *"We spoke earlier this year on the 3rd of March and you confirmed I had already saved you $XXX. I am sure that has continued and you have saved/gained far more by now – I am guessing around $XXX. Well, I am now at my year end and am just a little short of my target. Is there anything you need that I can help to deliver that will return that favour a little?"* And guess what, their orders came in, every year, on that very simple and completely unsophisticated basis. Now, I am absolutely not saying that is an appropriate tactic that all could or even should consider using, but you can see that the principle of identifying specific value has an enormous potential to help you – both with that customer and with then being able to reference what you have delivered to other parties as well. Hard results and numbers deliver a far more powerful message than the usual non-specific marketing phrases.

The Lesson
Always look for the value you can deliver, not just the product features. What will your solution actually do for them? How will it help them? Why should they buy from you – what's in it for them? Be as specific as you possibly can be. Almost no one does this, most use generalities...

"If you are not creating value for others you are wasting your time."
Bryant H McGill

Notes

Chapter 14 | Competition

"Think of business as a good game. Lots of competition and a minimum of rules. You keep the score with money..."

Bill Gates

Introduction

Competition is both a blessing and a curse. We vent when a competitor beats us, but we also exult when we are the winner. Make no mistake, it is competition that defines the market. As Nabil Jamal said, *"Competition in business is a blessing, for without it, we wouldn't be motivated to improve."* But how broad is your real competition? How difficult to overcome?

An Example

Competition and its impact have run through my career as a continual seam – for good and bad. We are taught about our direct marketplace competitors, we are briefed and updated on them and their weaknesses. But in my career, I have often lost to the 'hidden competitor'. I mean that in two very different senses. First, the actual competitor we didn't even know was competing until they had taken the deal from us and second, forms of competition that we didn't plan or sanity-check against. For example; *"We have decided to do nothing for the short term, but we may revisit it in the future"* or *"We have decided to soldier on with what we have".*

In dealing with our direct competitors we have plans and tactics we can adopt. Get in early and help to set the customer's agenda. Mention to the prospective customer the *"Three things the industry all agree are the most important criteria in this area"* (which of course also happen to be your three strongest solution capabilities ☺) and then perhaps even helping to influence or write their RFP document.

But what if you are late to the game? In this case, and if you believe you have a chance, you have to become a disruptor. Psychology theory taught me the principle of 'primacy and recency'. Whether you are one of a series of presenters on a specific day, looking at six potential new homes in one day or competing for a large B2B enterprise contract over a long period, being the first or last in are the best places to be. We are psychologically conditioned to notice – and remember - the first and last, with everything in the middle tending to be a bit of a blur. So being last does offer you a chance to a) ask those dumb questions about what the competitors have done to date, b) find out what the prospect hasn't liked so far and c) use your 'ignorance' to take a different approach from the others.

A very large institution was almost at the stage of changing all their admin systems to a competitor. The local team working for me decided to change everything. Over the course of just a week (the selection process had already been running for about four months) they dragged several very substantial systems into the institution, then held open, personal demonstrations for all admin staff and managers, literally hundreds of demos. Everyone was invited – and then made to feel important. Everyone was also asked what their main issues and frustrations were. That feedback then provided the genesis of the resultant, very simple proposal which highlighted several issues the RFP – and competitors - had not picked up on. The bid was then created, aided by some 'helpful comments' made by a few of those internally who had seen the competition and didn't like what they had seen. They felt we were more interested, more creative and more professional. The groundswell of support gained us a very substantial order and a long-term relationship with the institution.

So that's the situation with competitors. What about those other issues that can arise? I was at the end of a year-long process – where I had managed to out-manoeuvre the competition until I was the only one bidding – and had been told by my contact (once again ☹) that I would be getting the business. I went in to see the Financial Director of the company – a world renowned cargo company - to conclude things and he floored me by saying... *"I have decided not to go with the project. We need a number of new lorries and I have decided to spend the money on them instead – but thanks for your time and good work."*

I had wrongly assumed the only competition was internal to my project, but he, at his Board-level, had what is termed 'Discretionary Spend' – he could decide where the money he controlled was finally spent. And I had actually been competing with someone setting up a deal for a new fleet of lorries. That was a hard lesson, but a great piece of learning for the future. Later in my career, as MD of a substantial business, I then held those discretionary purse-strings. And yes, as I looked at what I would authorise spend on, I based my thinking on the relative value to me of each project that came across my desk (if there are lots of projects, sometimes they are measured and compared formally using IRR (Internal Rate of Return), TCO (Total Cost of Ownership), NPV (Net Present Value), impact on the balance sheet, CAPEX v OPEX etc). Every large-scale B2B deal will flow through Finance at some point. Always watch out for what else your customer or prospect could spend their money on. And in the depths of a project it's always worth asking your main contact exactly how they usually measure and analyse project spend and return and how they prioritise the use of their available funds. Match your proposal to what they say. If they reply with a term you don't know, just make a note and go in to your finance department or CFO when you get back to the office.

So, when looking at a major deal (and trying to qualify) ask yourself some serious questions;
- Could there be any direct competitors we haven't come across yet? Have we checked?
- Is there a 'normal' competitor missing?
- Is this project definitely ring fenced or could the spend be diverted elsewhere?
- Could the prospect do it themselves, or even wrongly believe they could do so?
- Have we proven the real, unique benefits and value we will deliver?
- How can we disrupt the other players?
- If you haven't found any competition – of any form - yet, then you do need to continually re-check to be sure.

Another thought, and this one is really a bit 'off the wall'. A concept was espoused in the late 1990's and early 2000's - for a short time. It was called 'coopetition'. The idea was that you sometimes sold against a strong competitor but then actively partnered with them in another venture when things aligned. So much for the theory... Three times in my career I have picked up the phone to a competitor who had beaten me well, in a straight and 'honourable' fight. They had done superbly, sold better than me and deserved their wins. So, I called them to tell them just that. All three were surprised but pleased to receive the call and we chatted about the deal and teased each other. Of course, I told them that the next time we met I would win! I didn't hear again from two of them but about a year after we spoke, I had a call from the third player. He had a good account that he was very close to. He explained that they had asked for a particular solution that he didn't have the power to deliver for them. He had remembered that my company did operate in that area, so he called to say he had already recommended me personally to them and provided an introduction. His customer was more than open as they already trusted him implicitly. After a very short campaign I gained a nice, high five figure deal. That net result came after just three short (and really fun!) phone calls. Not a bad use of my time...

Finally, when you look at your competitors – and your own relative strengths - also consider the 'teeth-to-butt ratio'. This phrase describes the life cycle and competitive effectiveness of companies. Let me explain; at Silicon Graphics, a great leader, Joe Dinucci, used this phrase to describe the evolution of all companies over time. When you start up your business (say two people) everyone sells and evangelises. You start to grow, but you are still a tight team, all dedicated to the same goal. Once you get to a certain point you need an administrator or two, then finance, then logistics, multiple management layers, HR etc. These organisations then develop their own sub-goals, processes and standards. Over time the 'teeth to butt' ratio moves downward from 100% to 70% then 35% etc. This happens to all companies through their lifecycle. Think of your own company overall or your branch/country operation. How many people out of the total employed <u>live or die</u> by their personal direct sales results? I would suggest that a country/branch operation should NEVER have less than 20% of staff directly goaled in selling. How does your organisation compare? And at the company level? Perhaps 10-12% should be the very 'worst'? As all companies evolve, they have less teeth pro rata and more and more 'butt'. Don't get me wrong, while the analogy is crude – and those job roles are truly required to help the company grow – the message is that as we do grow and evolve, we get slower and more bound by internal organisation and process. Even before I told this story you already knew it from your own experience. The biggest players in any sector are always under attack – and frequently outmanoeuvred – by smaller, nimbler competitors. The fate of those large, lumbering dinosaurs when attacked by the faster, smaller beasts is a feature of the movies, and very relevant to us in business.

The Lesson
Competition is a major factor in your success or failure. BUT you must look outside the box when considering your position and chance of winning. Don't be blindsided, make sure you do that to the other vendors!

> *"You can't look at the competition and say you're going to do it better. You have to look at the competition and say you're going to do it differently."*
> **Steve Jobs**

Notes

Chapter 15
Attitude in Your Business Life

"Attitude is a little thing that makes a big difference."

Winston Churchill

Introduction

Attitude can be a positive or negative force for us, throughout our life and in all our endeavours. You sometimes hear people say, about a colleague *"What a bad attitude they have"*. Of course, in selling, a positive attitude is really important. It isn't how often you are knocked down in life, it's how often you get back up again...

An Example

I was a very late surprise to my parents! My Father survived being in the first wave on D-Day. He then survived the whole British Army campaign through France and Germany including the liberation of Paris. I am sure that a combination of good fortune, very hard work and a positive attitude were crucial to his success. I can't imagine just how difficult it would be to have the right attitude in those situations – and he faced quite a few. When business situations seem challenging to me, I sometimes think of his journey and efforts and my issues don't seem quite so serious!

In selling, attitude comes to the fore mostly when we face adversity. I have seen colleagues lose it, stop trying or hit out when they have lost a major deal. Of course, the first thing to do is to be sure you really have lost. Has the order been completely finalised, is there something you could do to help them change direction or share the deal? If you have performed well, are there other needs you could help them with? But if you really have lost there are just two approaches to that situation. You can either 'go negative' or take a bit of time to yourself and ask – *"Well, I lost, but what did I learn from that experience that will help me to win in the future?"* You see, in the very act of losing, there is almost always a lesson that we can learn if we are focussed and humble enough to look for it. *"What did I do wrong? What did the competition do better? What did I forget to do? What could I have done differently?"* It is a bit of a cliché, but every failure brings you closer to success. In my opinion, one of the most common factors amongst the biggest winners is this very attitude.

Sometimes we are dissatisfied because we don't know everything; or have every element of the solution for the customer; or we just don't understand the situation perfectly. M J Wheatley, an author, is among those credited with the concept of 'dwelling in uncertainty'. In other words, do all you can, find out all you can, act to the best of your potential and then stop worrying! We have to do this all the time in our personal lives, but for some reason we often think we need a higher level of certainty in business. Chill. Just do what you can. Do it well. Lead from the front (see the next chapter). If you are competent and have a reasonable solution (it REALLY doesn't have to be the best) you have the ability to succeed. Why do I say this? Surely having the best features or services are critical to successful selling, aren't they?

Many years ago, it was felt by a number of commentators and industry players that at its peak (and as far and away the largest player in world-wide technology at the time – think perhaps of Microsoft and Apple combined today) – IBM, in many of the product and service areas they delivered into, did not have the absolute 'number 1' best technical solution available. If you were a disk manufacturer your disks might have better specs or faster access time than they did. The same for mid-range servers, office software, desktop computers etc. But they always had a solution or service that worked, did what it said it would do and a phenomenal attitude that drove them onwards and upwards. And I know. I competed against them directly for over 18 years and learned that lesson fast and hard! Why does this matter? The exact same applies today. You just do not need the largest list of features, or the number one rated product to win consistently. If your service or solution is functional, does the basics of what it should and is effective then you have enough. That's something we could all learn from.

Be different. The story is told of a salesperson working in a large organisation. She wanted to stand out internally because salespeople were looked down on by many in the company. So, every time she worked with administrators or needed their help, she treated them like internal customers. After every trip she would bring back something by way of a (very small) memento and chat to them about what she had done and learned. Step by step she gained their trust and support. THEN, having done this, she bought a box of bright pink paper. Now, every time she put in an internal request or submitted her expenses, she printed them on that paper. Instantly, the rest of the business knew that pink meant her. That was 'Pavlovian conditioning' (see Pavlov in the appendices). While colleagues had long delays in getting what they needed and even in getting their expenses paid, she found everything was going very smoothly for her! While paper might not be the medium today, you can surely see how this same principle could be applied in your world...

Take the high ground whenever you can. I don't know many prospects who enjoy hearing salespeople disparage their competition. As a senior executive, I personally found that approach uncomfortable to listen to. I tend towards the *"They are a good organisation with some reasonable solutions"* approach myself. Being more neutral and professional sets you apart from those that hit out at the competition. It also shows confidence in your own position. If directly attacked, just respond to the points raised, don't get into tit-for-tat in front of the customer. In the 'UK Apprentice' TV show I feel very uncomfortable when, at the end of each episode, the two or three who are up to be fired usually resort to insults and shouting to try to become the one that remains. First, it doesn't help them. Second, remaining calm and professional says a lot about you and your character. Again, do all you can. Do it to the best of your ability. Then chill.

And do say 'no' – internally and with those you sell to. Be honest. Rather than saying *"yes"* to everything, do say *"no"* if you can't, it will reduce the problems later down the track. Or even just say *"If I can, I will do it for you"*. Demand – as much as you can - that internal meetings have a start and finish time and an agenda covering everything that will be discussed. Make sure other factors inside your organisation don't eat too heavily into your selling time.

And integrity is one of the most valuable commodities you have, don't trade it for anything. Yes, it might cause you issues in the short term, and yes, compromising on what you believe is often easier. But you will be more successful – and like yourself a whole lot more – if you stick to your principles.

Don't ever be that 'seagull salesperson' we all hate. They fly in, dump 'you know what' all over everyone then leave the mess for others to deal with. There lies the path to career failure, no matter who you are and what you do. And while I am it, I have never seen long term results come from shouting, 'bulldozing' or intimidating. In work and in life, the soft spoken, clear, concise and logical should always trump raw emotion and threats. Of course, emotion has its uses, but it's not a philosophy for success on its own!

And finally, keep learning. What do you do, on at least a monthly basis, to improve your skills? Do you read books? Do you watch the News? Do you follow business publications? Do you listen to selling and business blogs or podcasts? While the world continues to move forward, if you stop learning, everyone else will start to move ahead of you – at least the competent professionals you have to worry about will. So, if you are interested in selling – keep learning. If you have been selling for five years – keep learning. If it's ten years, keep learning. And twenty, thirty and forty years... Always keep learning and growing.
As Henry Ford said, *"Anyone who stops learning is old, whether at twenty or eighty. Anyone who keeps learning*

stays young..." You can have a look at the appendices for some specific suggestions on this subject...

The Lesson
Your attitude says to others who you really are more than words could ever do. Make sure yours is consistently positive and based on personal integrity.

"For success, attitude is equally important as ability."

Sir Walter Scott

Notes

Chapter 16

Leading From the Front

"A leader is one who knows the way, goes the way, and shows the way."

John C Maxwell

Introduction
Some consider selling, particularly B2B, as a job for the lone maverick. I disagree. The most successful sales people I have met have all been true team players. A sign of confidence for a true leader is that they want to have the strongest people around them – they are not intimidated by pushback, experience or intelligence – they relish having that feedback and input. The same should apply for those who sell in the five, six and seven figures £/$/€ world. This is a complex activity and including and then leading great people to help you in the endeavour is far and away the best route to take.

An Example
In this book I have already talked about successful teams working to win business. Time and again I have seen this capability overcome massive opposition. The collective talent of a small team far outweighs the charismatic individual. But what can you do as a salesperson to create a team environment? My own industry has been known for a pretty much 'hire and fire' approach but I always believed in doing the right thing and leading from the front, rather than using the stick. That often made me 'different', but I wasn't concerned about that.

In my first sales management role I took over a branch that was bottom in the UK out of 49 branches. Not an easy task (but of course, in that situation the only way you can go is up!). I was told to maintain some distance from the team as their new manager, but I ended up actively involved in trying to work on and then help close every deal along with each salesperson – after all, keeping a distance had got the branch to this position. Looking back, I might now argue I actually did too much of that, but my belief at the time was that if they started to succeed individually, the branch would too. I was in before them, away after them and always available to help. I covered their backs with senior management as early forecasts dropped short. Over time we actually became a real team. We won and lost together. We started to want to achieve for each other. This may sound corny, but one of the nicest moments in my 40+ year career was when, after a particularly important month ended with us missing target – yet again – and I had been beaten up by senior management – yet again – we were having a bite of lunch and one of the guys quietly handed me an envelope. I opened it up and it was an apology card signed by everyone in the sales and pre-sales team saying they were really sorry, and it wouldn't happen again. We had bonded, and they felt for my situation and for me. Fast forward nine months and the UK monthly newsletter (which I still have a copy of) had a note from the UK Sales Director saying *"...and finally, could any other branch than X please win the monthly league table, it's getting boring..."* Yes, we had gone from 49th to top. The team was performing. As a salesperson you too should be leading a team – pre-sales, technical, customer services, managers and executives. Get them working for and with you.

As you work to create a team, psychology theory talks (correctly in my experience) about the four stages of team development (original source: Bruce Tuckman) -
Forming → Storming → Norming → Performing...

1. **Forming.** Coming together. Getting a name or some group identity (even if it's temporary). Beginning to understand each other and what the overall goal and their roles are. Led by the leader – you.
2. **Storming.** Where everyone tries to find their place in the team. Lots of discussion, argument, ideas, feedback. Everyone involved.
3. **Norming.** The roles and actions are established, everyone knows each other and what to do. Not perfect but definitely getting there. Functioning together.
4. **Performing.** This is where that first team got to. A real team 'engine' that has an expectation of winning and excelling, both internally and externally. 'Flying'.

Where are you and your 'team' in this development/process right now? (And it may not be a formal team but one you have pulled together just for that deal or bid.)

The Lesson
I have seen plenty more examples throughout my career that make me certain of this method of working. The message is this. If you take the lead and involve others (even those not directly involved) your chances of success increase dramatically. Teams do better than individuals and, as a B2B salesperson, you should be a team leader. Now, your business card might not say that you are a 'leader', but you need to become one in order to succeed.

"Leadership is a choice, not a position."

Stephen R Covey

Notes

Chapter

17

Selling in the World of Subscription Pricing

"The secret of change is to focus all of your energy not on fighting the old, but on building the new."

Socrates

Introduction

I have had recent experience of salespeople who are used to 'big ticket' capital sales struggling to adapt to the 'new idea' of subscription pricing/cloud-based business models – like SaaS (Software as a Service). This section may become rather dated as the trend is gathering pace as I write it and subscription models may become the de facto norm in every geography and market sector soon enough anyway but there is also an underpinning message about coping with change to be discussed...

An Example

When buying goods personally you can take the capital approach – buy it for cash - or look at annuity or subscription pricing options (mortgages, car leases or rentals for example). In the consumer world, the idea of spreading cost is well established. Historically, in business, organisations would look to purchase outright (if the pricing was good and/or if it suited them to take a depreciating asset onto their books – usually for tax allowance benefit) or lease/rent the item instead (if conserving cash was the best route to go and increasing their asset base and reducing tax through capital allowances wasn't the right thing to do). In my career, the largest items like mainframes, at seven figure sums, were very often leased.

But it was the norm, more often than not, across all markets, for high value capital goods (the hint is in the title ☺) to be bought outright. Today we see a great cross-industry move worldwide towards rental, lease or straight forward subscription payment schemes. At the lowest level we can see how Microsoft have moved from capital pricing for one-user home 'Office' (at say $250) to a subscription model with Office 365 at $10 or so per month. Why are they doing this at the retail level? It all comes down to them gaining a higher 'LTV' – Long Term Value. At the higher, corporate level, particularly in technology with cloud computing solutions that are created by the vendor but then hosted and managed by others (like Amazon

AWS and Microsoft Azure) we see that the norm is solidly based on monthly or quarterly payments now. Commercial planes are rarely bought now as they traditionally were, they are almost always leased – so that the finances can be 'matched' (outgoings are covered by revenues, plus profit to the airline, the big capital payment 'lumps' are removed). For the salesperson used to closing deals at say $500K or above, it can be difficult to get excited about $15K monthly. But after just four years that $15K has delivered $720K revenue...

I was once (at a sales kick off meeting) privileged to hear a speaker from the then self-proclaimed 'World's best supermarket'. The small, local supermarket group (today with six stores in New York State and Connecticut) was called Stew Leonards. They coined their two rules of business which have become famous all over the world since they introduced it. They believed in it so much they carved it on a 3-ton stone outside their first store –

Rule 1. The customer is always right
Rule 2. If the customer is ever wrong, reread rule 1

And they actually meant it...

Major, large name competitors put in their best store managers from elsewhere and offered special pricing and offers against them, but none could dent their position in the local market. A Director in our company (who had sponsored the talk) told how he and his young family had moved to a new house and arrived with nothing to eat. Late at night he and his family found Stew Leonards and bought a <u>very</u> large basket of food. At the till he realised he had left his wallet in his new home. *"No problem"* said the teller, *"Here's the receipt, pop back when you are sorted and pay us then".* Could you imagine your local supermarket teller having that ability or authority? The speaker told us the story of a customer who broke a tooth on a baguette they had sold. They came in and asked if the carving on the stone outside was true. The supervisor said *"Yes". "Well, here's the bill for $200 to fix the tooth"* - and they paid it! The loyalty they generated from their customers was incredible. Nothing anyone else did could persuade them to go elsewhere. Imagine being a big player's store manager being parachuted in to this area to 'sort things out' – how could you compete? If you were 3% cheaper for a few weeks would the local population drop a retailer like that and move to you?

In that talk, our guest speaker then mentioned the concept of valuing the customer. He explained that *"If a customer with a bill for $25 is complaining, don't get upset about the $25 and what they want fixed compared to it, even if it costs far more. Imagine they have a post-it note stuck to their forehead with $104,000 on it. That's what the average customer will spend here ($100 a week) over 20 years, not to mention all their family, friends and colleagues added on top!"*

I left the presentation reeling. The power of that attitude was almost impossible for me to describe. Everyone in the business could decide themselves what was the right thing to do to make the customer happy and customers were considered based on their lifetime potential. Did it work? Well, the company was incredibly profitable too. In 1992, Stew Leonard's earned an entry into The Guinness Book of World Records for having *"the greatest sales per unit area of any single food store in the United States."* Do look them up and read their story...

That's how we should approach subscription-based opportunities. What does this deliver to us over three or five years or longer? How likely are we to get more add-ons or upgrades? How can we make it even easier for the prospect? Does this regular relationship enable us to do more for and with the customer?

Subscription based selling is still exactly the same selling, it's just that the delivery mechanism for payment has changed.

It's also not new. In my own industry I have seen several cycles over the years. Today software vendors talk about flexible applications. Previously it was apparently 'all less flexible' – the customer had to fit their 'solution'. Yet, in the 1970's (!) we sold our very basic accounting systems based on the 'parameter driven' options we gave our customers, that enabled them to fit our solution to their needs – pretty well exactly. Computing was centralised (through mainframes), then over time it became dispersed through the introduction of minicomputers, then PC's, departmental servers etc. Today it is rapidly becoming centralised again (what do you think cloud computing is, if not centralised operations?) So, in every market sector, things do change, then change back again – and in every aspect of life, over time.

The Lesson
Don't be phased because things are different. They are still more as they were than they are changed. But if we can't change the world, then we have to change to fit the new world. Over my 40+ years in technology the direction of travel, solution approach and architectures have moved back and forward many times. Embrace it and enjoy it!

"There is nothing permanent except change."

Heraclitus

Notes

Chapter 18

Negotiation

"During a negotiation, it would be wise not to take anything personally. If you leave personalities out of it, you will be able to see opportunities more objectively."

Brian Koslow

Introduction
Negotiation, like qualification, is one of the fundamental skills in selling. Once you are in serious discussions, negotiation comes into play. Not just at the end of the process, but throughout. This chapter discusses just a few aspects of negotiation that you need to plan for and work into your sales process.

Example
Negotiation is part of all of our lives. *"Sam. Stop playing and let's go now and see Granny"* (we all know exactly how those conversations go if the child is happy where he/she is!). You want to go to a specific restaurant but of course you say to your wife/husband/partner/friend *"Tom, when we are out tonight where should we eat?"* – and you then try to move the conversation to what you want. ;) *"Beth, I know you want to buy our enterprise product, but I understand you feel the price is too high. Can we discuss how we can reach agreement?"*. All of these are examples of the commencement of a negotiation process.

It is said by some business gurus that selling is a 'game'. Negotiation is at the pinnacle of that gaming process. Looked at from above, any negotiation falls into distinct phases and steps – and we need to understand what these are and then prepare for the ultimate negotiation that will undoubtedly follow. Not planning or preparing - and then just falling into a final negotiation to close the deal - is a recipe for expensive failure. This short commentary does not pretend to teach all of negotiation theory, steps and tactics, I just want to give some pointers. For further detailed research there are a host of sources. Entering 'negotiation process' into Google results in 366 million hits! There are literally hundreds of thousands (or more) of detailed presentations, graphics, articles, videos and images! All follow a generally similar theme with some variations, so what follows is the way I view this broad landscape.

First, to be prepared to negotiate to win the deal you need to understand the customer dynamics, their situation and drivers, their personalities and 'wins'. To best succeed you need to find these out at both the personal and corporate level – as they may very well not match. This requires research (as discussed earlier) and a continual desire to find (and then re-check and restate) their stated goals and drivers. Before 'selling' you need to undergo this process. If there isn't a strong fit with your solution capability, why are you there anyway? This is the first step to being prepared to negotiate.

Second, one goal throughout your sales cycle is to find, agree and 'bank' as many areas for later discussion and agreement as possible. Sophisticated buyers will always aim to narrow down to just one element – most commonly price. Once they have done this, they have a powerful ability to play potential suppliers off against each other – even where each vendor's offerings are very different. So, the critical goal for you is to ensure there are a number of agreed different factors in the decision. You need to establish all of their decision criteria. These could form a very long list of items specific to the situation - like your ability to increase their profits through your solution and services (and by how much?), your/your offering's reliability – and its impact on them, your experience and ability to consistently deliver, warranty, speed of project execution (which will, in turn deliver the benefits you provide faster), the resources to be deployed for them etc. With 10 minutes and a sheet of paper I am sure you could write down maybe 5-10 areas that might differentiate you from the competition and be worthy of consideration, be critical to their project success or that will be of particular interest to the buyer.

At this point it is critical that you then lay out and agree with the customer ALL of the points that you believe are up for negotiation. You have done your research and should be quite close. BUT this step is important to ensure you do have that full agreement with them. Why? I have found (to my cost) that, right at the very end of the negotiation with a serious professional – as you might see it – the buyer suddenly says that *"This is all good, but..."* and adds in another extra one or two items after you have reached what you thought was your final point of agreement. This is a powerful buyer's technique and puts you at a major disadvantage. Clearly confirming ALL elements of the final negotiation up front should help towards removing that likelihood.

It is then important that you sell/persuade/pre-negotiate with the prospect to the point that they accept, even just conversationally, that you deliver something different and also equivalent or hopefully better in at least some of the areas you have discussed. You MUST also agree what is critical to them, and what is less so. Again, you must also agree what is 'in and out' of the final decision criteria so you know what you are working with. It is an interesting fact, that if you do this (and keep notes) when you come to that inevitable point of disagreement in the detail of the final negotiation and you say *"But on the 20th you told me..."* (referring directly to those notes) very few individuals will then just ignore that fact to your face. Rather, they will try to work around or justify it – and you have gained a small edge. All of this will, of course, involve both selling, listening and negotiation skills throughout...

As you enter the final, and crucial phase of negotiation you should then have some form of agreement on what the decision criteria are. You know all the elements that are important to them, and you know what is important to you. You have now set the basis for a reasonable negotiation. Trying to negotiate on just one area – like price – is incredibly difficult and ultimately unsatisfying. Offered the choice between a bad deal or a catastrophic one (very high discount given or losing the deal, for example) everyone will choose the bad deal. That's the game the buyer wants you to play. But it is usually not the only option if you have taken the above steps...

You are now better prepared to enter into the detail of that game and process...

Before you meet or call them consider the following –
- List all of the elements and factors you have found
- Sort them into 'must haves', 'negotiable' and 'not important' – preferably on both sides
- Decide what is the order of trades you would be willing to carry out on the latter two categories (in other words what is easiest to trade, second easiest etc)
- Set your absolute 'no further' red lines on all items. Then make your decision before you go in - what would not be worth giving up or going to in order to win the deal
- What might you ask for as a trade at the final negotiation point? A favourite of mine is a written confirmation that they will provide an open (all media forms) reference and/or host an agreed number of on-site visits for other prospective customers
- Decide your plan for the discussion
- Stick to it!

The greatest issue I have seen time and again in negotiation is that people, in the heat of the moment, and with the deal 'so close', get to a point where they give away far more than they would have done in the bright light of day. A week later they are disappointed, unhappy with the deal and perhaps fighting with their management. Take the emotion out of it and decide beforehand EXACTLY where your bottom line is.

Once you have done all of that, you can actually enjoy the game that follows. You know what you bring (and hopefully its value to them), you know what they need and their priorities, you know the elements you can trade off to gain a deal. With all of that you are well set to win! (or should I say win/win!).

How do you know the negotiation has concluded successfully for both parties? Well, first the obvious evidence should be there – both parties are happy with the outcome and continue to engage. Where the outcome is win/lose then one party will be ecstatic, the other upset and simply not happy. In this case – often associated with the more aggressive 'one hit' school of selling – the salesperson might win the battle but will almost always go on to lose the war. The customer will go out of their way either to not do more business with them, or will aim to reverse the situation next time round. Lost in the mists of my own history is a phrase I remember from a 'guru' who said the best negotiation leaves both parties happy but just ever so slightly disappointed they didn't get a bit more. I can see what they were saying!

Take every opportunity to practice. Haggling with a market trader or car salesman prepares you and tunes your abilities. Maybe that learning will help you close a strategic deal two years later. If you are uncomfortable negotiating at this level, how will you then sell successfully against serious corporate negotiators?

The Lesson
In the same way that you would plan ahead for a long journey, or to do something important for the first time, you must plan before negotiating. Lose the emotion, think of the facts, really understand both sides and then plan for the process itself.

"Before a negotiation can proceed and be completed, what is outside the scope of negotiation needs to be agreed."

Christine Lagarde

Notes

Chapter 19
Focus on Your Priorities

"Concentrate all your thoughts upon the work at hand. The sun's rays do not burn until brought to a focus."

Alexander Graham Bell

Introduction
When the pressure is on, there is never enough time to do everything. For the salesperson who has a quota target to reach, that lack of time becomes dangerous and ever more critical as time passes. So how do we focus on the right things?

An Example
We can easily fill our time with nothing, or things that are less useful. Or even things that seem to be worth doing. Discussing this issue, the world-famous business guru, Stephen R Covey, once said *"Most of us spend too much time on what is urgent and not enough time on what is important..."* It is obvious that we need to prioritise.

The whole idea of priorities and focus is an interesting one. In my 40's and having gone straight to work from school I decided I should get some higher education. I opted to do a part time MBA (this involved one afternoon and evening up to 10:00pm every week at my local university in Edinburgh, plus almost every weekend, for three years, plus extra time back at work every week to cover those missing hours. It was great when it stopped!). One lecturer was teaching on the subject of priorities and he gave an analogy to explain <u>really</u> understanding priorities... *"Imagine you are on a commercial flight, crossing the Pacific. Exactly half way across with no land within 2,000 miles of you, the Captain tells you the engines are failing, and you will have to ditch! As you glide down towards the ocean there can only be one thought in your head... "Please let us 'land' safely". Somehow, miraculously, the sea is fairly calm, and the plane does indeed land and float for a few minutes. You get your lifejacket on and join the queue to jump into the sea. Again, there can only be one thought in your head... "Please let the lifejacket inflate". You jump and it does! The plane sinks, and you are now floating, legs down in the Pacific, with no rescue in sight. Now again there is only one possible thought "Please, no sharks!". And that is how priorities work. When you were gliding downwards in the plane, the lifejacket didn't actually matter. When you were just leaving the plane, sharks didn't matter..."* That lecture has stayed with me for 20+ years, what a message...

By way of another example, look up 'Maslow's Hierarchy of Needs'. This well-regarded research also points to a hierarchy in what we need to have in life (add 'Business' to the search and you will find multiple images of its application). If you haven't covered the basics then 'nice to haves' are of no interest. It powerfully applies to selling too!

How should these principles apply to us as we sell?

First don't focus on the urgent, focus on the important! To do that you actually need to have decided what your goal(s) are. So, decide them first. For every activity you might be asked to do, say to yourself, *"Does it help me achieve my goal(s)? If not, why am I doing it? If I have to do it, can I do it later or outside core working hours?"*

Second, you can have too many goals. If you have 15 goals, you will never be able to set those priorities effectively and benefit from the focus you should have. It has been said that all the greatest inventions and businesses in the world have been achieved by a 'Monomaniac on a Mission' (credited to Peter Drucker). Think of any great salesperson, business, political or religious leader. They all have that absolute focus on their goal and priorities. Nothing else gets in the way.

Finally, the principle of applying focus and priorities should apply to all aspects of your life, not just to business...

The Lesson
Know where you are going. Decide on your goals. Then set your priorities and work through them. Put to the side or delay anything that moves you away from those priorities!

"The successful warrior is the average person, with laser-like focus."

Bruce Lee

Notes

Chapter 20
Attitude in Your Personal Life

"Desires dictate our priorities, priorities shape our choices, and choices determine our actions."

Dallin H Oaks

Introduction
This book is, as you know if you have read this far, devoted to my business experiences and learning. But in this chapter I want to change the focus. I want to get personal and talk about my attitude to life outside work. You can smile at what follows, ignore it or think about it and hopefully take it into your own life. So, having 'finished' the book I really felt strongly that I wasn't done yet. The personal angle and the critical nature of life outside work also needs to be covered. What follows is a set of ideas and thoughts and I hope at least one hits home to you. So here goes...

An Example (or quite a few in this case!)
You might think that work is the most important thing, but it's not in the top three in my view. Through my own life and its successes <u>and failures</u> I really believe that your family and your own well-being should always come before work. Faith should also be higher rated, if you have a belief system you follow. With that solid base to your life you can then put in the right and appropriate time, focus and effort to work. Work should always be a means, not an end in itself.

Many years ago, I was driving and listening to BBC Radio. The news programme had a 'Thought for the Day' delivered each day by a different religious or moral leader. On this day, the speaker had been the manager of one of the UK's largest hospices – someone who had literally helped many thousands of people come to terms with and prepare for the end of their life. A fantastic life's work dedicated to helping others. After his 2-minute talk was finished the newsreader broke with tradition (usually just moving straight back to the news with no comment) and asked him if he had any other thoughts. The speaker thought for a second then just said *"Well, I can say this. Of all the people I have met over the past 20 years as they came to the end of their lives, not one has ever said "I wish I had spent more time in the office'..." Step back and really ask yourself,*

"What are my true priorities?".

As I write this 'extra' chapter it is a few days after Christmas. My first thought today is about a memory I will always carry with me from Christmas time. I mentioned my Father in Chapter 15. I was raised in a loving, stable but really quite poor family. Having survived WWII my Dad worked 'on the buses' as a conductor, then he became an Assistant Janitor in a local school, ending his life working as a Head Janitor in a large school. I never lacked for anything but can see, looking back, just how hard things were financially for my parents. At the time, of course, I didn't notice.

One Christmas things were obviously bad. I was small – I guess somewhere between seven and nine years old. I had one present. It was wrapped in plain brown paper. When I opened it, I realised it was a hand carved and then painted basic wooden boat. Very simple, but it must have taken hours to craft by hand. I was upset and didn't say thanks or ever use it. Now, looking back, as a parent and grandad myself, I realise that it was all they could give – and my Dad had taken the hours to make it himself – what an expression of love! And I rejected it.... My Dad died young, before we had any children and I would then come to realise just how important that interaction was. As I look back, if I still had that crude little carving, it would be pride of place, right in the centre of my home today. I wasn't grateful or gracious and how I regret that action to this day.

My Mum then lived for her later years (15 more after my Dad passed away) in what is known in the UK as 'Sheltered Housing' (termed 'assisted living' in the USA). She had her own apartment and complete freedom but had an alarm system in her home to get help if she needed. My wife and I and our children got on very well with 'Wee Granny'. She was incredibly fit and active. She would often say she was *"Busy running around getting in food and other supplies for the old folks."* We would reply *"But you are one of the old folks!"*

I too was very busy with work and life. We had talked several times over a month or two about going out together for a Chinese meal – something she had really started to enjoy as she got older. But I was always too busy and put it off. Then, one morning, I was contacted and told she had gone to sleep after a busy day and just hadn't wakened again. That meal and company she wanted would never now happen...

These two very, very big lessons taught me the importance of being grateful for everything, no matter how small and also in putting family first. And I haven't always succeeded in achieving this by any means. It doesn't matter if a thought, action or gift isn't quite right for you – acknowledge their action towards you properly and fully. And do take the opportunity to do those things for your closest family that you sometimes put off 'for another day'. For my part, it was the worst possible way to learn those lessons and so I commend them to you, so you don't have those regrets in your life.

(Postscript: This paragraph is added – out of sequence – as the book goes to print several months after all the other text has been completed and proofed. I thought I had two major life experiences to talk about, it turns out there were actually three, I just didn't know it yet! When I was young my older brother Mike and my sister Patricia both emigrated to Canada (I was younger and didn't). This year I was invited to my Nephew's wedding. It was one of those will I/won't I moments. With the above two stories in mind I decided to make the journey and my daughter and I headed to Alberta. I stayed with another nephew and his lovely wife, we caught up with all the family and very much enjoyed the wedding itself. In particular, my brother Mike and I enjoyed our mutual company several times, catching up after 10 years of physical separation. It was lovely. Then, almost four weeks to the day after our return home, I was

woken early in the morning to be told Mike had been found dead that day. The shock and grieving were dreadful but at least we had spent that time together. We had laughed about our childhood; we had renewed our brotherly friendship. It too, was time I could never get back again. But this time I had those great new memories and events to remember so fondly. How would I have felt had I decided it wasn't worth all that travel to go to the wedding?)

I know it is a trite phrase, but saying thanks is a simple and much underestimated thing to do. Your partner, family, friends and colleagues all need to know that you appreciate what they have done – or tried to do. Never miss that opportunity...

And that brings me nicely onto my next point. While I tell these two (now three) stories and acknowledge them, I also want to say that you should never spend your life looking back. It is good to remember and to learn from life as you go along. BUT you can't change the past, you can't alter history. The only time you have is right now. Tomorrow might not happen – as incidents and accidents we see on the news every day teach us – but today is yours for the taking. Life can be hard and unfair, but it is in how you react, not in what happens to you, that you develop and grow as a person. Learn the lesson and move on. Don't hold on to grudges or history in business or outside it. If knocked down, smile, stand back up and go forward again.

Be true to yourself. In all aspects of life, be you. Don't follow the crowd or a trend if it feels wrong for you. Those who love or like you will remain alongside you even if you are out of step. And the others? They just don't matter...

I like the principle of going the extra mile. In those societies invaded and then ruled by the Romans, each local citizen HAD to carry a backpack for a Roman soldier up to a mile if they asked/demanded. The whole concept of 'going the extra mile' takes on much stronger significance when you consider its origin from this diktat and how it must have felt to those subjected to it. In my personal life I have always tried (and very often failed) to do this. If something is asked of you and you actually can do it, be gracious and say *"Yes"* and then try to do a bit more as well.

You can either keep your head down and mutter a bit at life's travails or you can keep your head up and try to smile, no matter what your current circumstances are. I know which one makes you feel better, never mind others around you...

The story is told of a King who desperately wanted a simple motto for all of his life. He asked his advisors and working together, they couldn't think of anything. He extended the search, getting wise men to come to him from all parts of the kingdom. Still nothing. Finally, in desperation, he heard about a hermit who lived on top of the highest mountain at the furthest point of the Kingdom. He set out to meet with him and, after many weeks, arrived at his destination. Sitting at his feet he asked him *"What is the greatest motto for life?"*. The hermit thought for a while then said, *"This too will pass."* I have told this story countless times because I believe it to be so true – and important! If all is great for you, life couldn't be better, and all is well then just be aware that 'This too will pass'. If everything is on top of you and just can't get any worse then *"This too will pass"*. If things are just muddling along, neither dreadful nor fantastic then, guess what, *"This too will pass"*. Those four words can describe my whole life to date. And I bet they encapsulate yours too...

Finally, I was reading online and saw a fantastic comment on an open forum that I want to share with you. Often in life and in work we sometimes feel we just don't have the talent to achieve what we desire. Molly Fletcher, a US-based motivational speaker and thought leader recently said the following –

"Here are 10 things that require zero talent –

1. Being on time
2. Work ethic
3. Effort
4. Body language
5. Energy
6. Attitude
7. Passion
8. Being coachable
9. Doing extra
10. Being prepared"

Just how far would those attributes take you even if you had zero talent or aptitude?

The Lesson
Be yourself. Be grateful. Be honest. Be helpful. Think of others. Live for today, not the past or the future...

"Your days are numbered. Use them to throw open the windows of your soul to the sun. If you do not, the sun will soon set, and you with it."

Marcus Aurelius

Notes

Chapter 21 | Summary and Conclusion

"After all is said and done, there's always more said than done..."

Aesop (slightly adapted)

Introduction
Well here we are. At the beginning of the book I said that I wanted to pass on my experience – good and bad – to help others who are already in or moving into high-value, B2B sales. I really hope I have succeeded! ☺

Thoughts
What would I regard as success? If all of the book did nothing for you, <u>except</u> for one single idea or tactic which helps you to improve how you sell, or live your life, then I am happy. Out of 21 chapters I hope at least something has resonated with you. Along the way I hope you have found the book to be absolutely 'non-textbook' in style as promised, easy to read, perhaps funny in places and informative. I hope you have read stories that you can learn from and even pass on to others at the right time.

If you are one of the characters I have mentioned, you will know who you are! And my career has certainly been punctuated by some very real characters and fantastic experiences.

I would hope that you can take some time to yourself and consider these concepts. At even just a chapter a day there should be lessons in here for everyone. After 40+ years in business I too was remembering and re-learning as I went along in writing this book. If you are highly experienced, I do hope that this has served as a reminder for you. We can all do with taking time out to refresh our knowledge.

What are the main lessons? I wrote this book from a perspective of things that I thought might be useful to others. But the content was in no way pre-planned, it literally just flowed as I typed. Reading it back to myself I would say there are perhaps 10 main themes to my experience and learning over all these years -

- Be true to yourself. You will find that approach and 'repeatable method' that works well for you in business and in life

- The only place success comes before work is in the Dictionary

- Be creative, but where needed (like in qualification or negotiation) always plan and follow a process

- Always try to think and act outside the box

- Keep learning! Read, listen, watch, try...

- The most successful players all compete against themselves to improve, not just against others

- Never be afraid to ask questions. It shows you are interested and it's the best way to find out more!

- Succeed by working with others. Value them and thank them as you go along

- Do the right thing. Be honest and have integrity. No matter what today says, you will be happier – and more successful – in the long term

- How you act always defines you more than any words you can say

The Lesson
But those are my thoughts. So, here's the challenge to you. Why not take a few minutes and think of just three things you have read about in this book? Which ideas struck you as the most useful? How could you now use these 'Top Three' skills or techniques in your career? How will you start to use them – and when?

Idea 1 _____

_____

Idea 2 _____

_____

Idea 3 _____

_____

I thank you for taking the time to read the book (or even parts of it). I wish you good luck, but more important, great success, for the future...

Jim Irving
January 2020

Appendix 1

Some quotes about the author

(These are a broader sample of quotes and also include the full comments which are shown summarised in the preface to this book)

"A key objective for any company is revenue growth, the outcome of which lies in the hands of relatively few people - your sales team. Transforming sales performance needs someone with the insight to understand your vision and the practical know-how to deliver on it. Experienced leadership and people skills are the keys to this and Jim Irving is one of the select band of individuals with both qualities. He has a long track record of making a real difference where it matters most - the bottom line."

Jim Green, CEO and Co-Founder, Spartan Solutions

"Jim is an excellent leader who manages to combine the strength of character, determination and toughness that's required to fulfil senior roles with his great kindness, warmth and humility. He also brings his huge experience and wealth of skills to bear in a hands-on manner and was an excellent manager to work for. I would gladly recommend him to anyone."

Gary Baverstock, Sales Director Northern Europe, Denodo Technologies

"The most difficult challenge in business is to make simplicity out of complexity. Jim is one of those few who can make any process seem simple. His methodical and diligent approach to the sales process and every sales cycle is why he has seen and passed on so much success."

Ryan McAnlis, Former CEO, JAR Technologies

"I first met Jim when I asked him to be the MD of a technology company I chaired. He brought clarity and strong execution to the business and massively increased market visibility while improving business results and motivating staff. He delivers very strong sales and communication skills to every endeavour"

Michael Black MBE. Successful technology entrepreneur. Non-Exec Director at Danske Bank, Non-Exec Director at Titan IC Systems and Chairman – Displaynote Technologies

"Jim is a seasoned sales leader with a proven track record of success in multiple channels and business models. His leadership and motivation skills elevate the productivity of his teams resulting in consistently exceeded goals. He is respected by his customers, team, peers, and senior management."

Greg Goelz, President and CEO, Smart Locus Inc, California

"I have known Jim for over 25 years now. We have not worked in business together, but I do know him very well personally. I know of his career success, both in the UK and internationally and his honest and ethical approach to selling. Jim is a strong mentor and communicator and he is an excellent and motivating speaker."

Stephen Kerr, Member of the UK Parliament and Member of the UK Select Committee on Business, Energy and Industrial Strategy. Also, Parliamentary Adviser to the Association of Professional Sales

"Jim is one of those few people who has a real presence… This credible presence and his great persuading and influencing skills are invaluable when communicating at the highest levels within the organisation…."

Chief Data Officer, UK Top 3 FTSE Company

"Jim's reputation is very well established. He has gone in to lead sales/the business in difficult circumstances and markets and has delivered clarity in strategy and also in sales execution and improved results. He understands the dynamics of selling."

Professor Paul Atkinson, Founding Partner - Par Equity (a multi award winning VC firm), Executive Chairman Taranata Group and serial investor.

"As a specialist IT lawyer with over 40 years' experience both in private practice and in-house, I have acted for IT businesses from start-ups to large multi-nationals. I have seen the very best and the very worst of sales performances. In Jim's book I have found countless echoes of my own experiences and commercial encounters. I found myself nodding in agreement on almost every page. This book will be of great value to any salesperson at any stage of their careers - excellent advice for the beginner, and a timely aide-memoire for the experienced. I commend it."

Paul Klinger LLB, Solicitor. Former Director of Legal Services, EMEA, at Silicon Graphics, Inc.

"Turning around a broken sales organization, one with a culture of underperformance and lethargy is a monumental challenge. At Information Builders, in short order, Jim took a bottom-dwelling country operation and grew it to one of the best performing teams in the world. His no-frills, straightforward and ethical approach to building a world-class sales organization is something to this day that I not only admire, but also strive to emulate."

David Rode. Former Senior Vice President, International Operations, Information Builders (IBI)

Appendix 2

A listing of resources that might be helpful to you. (All comments are the authors own)

This chapter contains my own, personal opinions. Any errors in facts or description are entirely mine!

Books
I have been reading and learning more about sales from books, articles, and more recently blogs and webinars, for over 40 years. The following selection is in no particular order of merit. It is just a list of some great books and other resources that I believe are worth looking into...

1. **Selling to VITO (Very Important Top Officer)** by Anthony Parinello. An oldie but very powerful...

2. **You can Negotiate Anything** and several others by Herb Cohen. Negotiation approach, skills and techniques from the undisputed master...

3. **Sales EQ, Fanatical Prospecting** and **Objections** – all by Jeb Blount. A great writer...

4. **Business Impact Selling** by Sue Aspinall. A focus on 'Business Outcomes' using easy to implement techniques and skills from the founder of Exceed Global.

5. **SPIN Selling** by Neil Rackham. A sales classic. A simple methodology for high value product and services sales...

6. **The Little Red Book of Selling** by Jeffrey Gitomer. A very unusual and challenging book – which I enjoyed! Mixed B2C and B2B...

7. **Stop Selling, Start Partnering** by Larry Wilson. This is REALLY old – my copy is dated 1994! It talks about planning and understanding first and then helping the customer and is ageless in that respect. It aims to help you retain and grow customers for the long term.

8. **The New Conceptual Selling** by Miller Heiman. One of the standard bibles of corporate selling. Also, The new Strategic Selling – a companion book by the same authors.

9. **Solution Selling** by Michael Bosworth. Another classic about the process of corporate selling...

10. **The New Power Base Selling** by Jim Holden. An updated version of an older but extremely powerful best-selling book...

11. **The Challenger Sale** by Matthew Dixon. A serious bestseller, focused on challenging your prospect/customer, not just learning about them...

12. **Secrets of Successful Sales** by Alison Edgar. This UK based 'Entrepreneur's Godmother' is a great read with lots of tips...

Other Materials
Almost all of the above authors have blogs – and all are worth dipping into. Several, including Herb Cohen, are featured heavily on YouTube and Linkedin for your viewing and listening pleasure...

Also look at Linkedin, YouTube and elsewhere for blogs and channels on professional selling. Some are good, some bad, some excellent... Also, for broadening your knowledge more generally, consider the free/low cost sources of information on a vast range of subjects like Alison.com, the Open University, udemy.com, edx.org and many others. Or go to the 'mother website' for this type of learning to start with – www.mooc.org (Massive Open Online Courses)...

Appendix 3

Sample Sales Process and 'Ratios' forms

This appendix relates to chapter four, 'Follow the Numbers'. In that chapter I described the process of analysing your relative success in the various stages of your sales process through the use of ratios.

It is worth mentioning that many 'sales manuals' set out the definitive sales process and steps. I believe they are all partly true but are also all equally flawed. The steps in your sales process – depending on your industry, expectations, traditions, product, solution or service offerings and also to some extent, your customers – will be different from others. There is no single 'perfect sales process flow' in my experience. But I would expect you to be able to clearly define between four to seven stages in most markets. In order to use a ratios-based approach you need to first understand and confirm the steps in your own process. This review stage is also a good point at which to review the success of your organisation's approach and sales methodology/process. In the light of an undoubtedly changing external environment are the accepted stages still the right ones?

Step 1 – Your Sales Stages

In this step, note down the clear, consistent and definable stages in your sales process. I have included an example of a possible first step definition...

OUR SALES STAGES DEFINITION – "ACME Inc"

Stage and Name	Description/Definition
1. "First Contact" or "Cold Call"	A successful cold call, response to a social media contact or inbound lead received, leading to stage 2.
2.	
3.	
4.	
5.	
6.	
7.	
8.	

Step 2 - History

The next step is to look at recent history. Be honest with yourself and use real data. If none exists then start to keep records for at least a month before completing this stage. I would suggest a month is the bare minimum. The example below shows an annual history. Longer is always better for analytical and accuracy purposes -

HISTORIC ANALYSIS – OVER XXXXX PERIOD (Month, quarter or year)

Stage Name and Number	Numbers Achieved	Ratio Achieved
1. Cold Call	7,600	N/A
2. First Meeting	950	8:1
3. Second Meeting and Demo	230	4:1
etc.	etc.	etc.

Step 3 – Reviewing Your Own Performance

Once you have defined your sales stages and measured the previous experience and results you can then monitor your ongoing results against your own target very easily. This time I show a sample of a monthly version – but quarterly and annual would be exactly the same...

SALES STAGES AND RATIO PERFORMANCE IN DECEMBER 2019

Stage Name and Number	Monthly Target	Target Ratio	Actual Achieved	Actual Ratio
1. Cold Call	640	N/A	597	N/A
2. First Qualified Meeting/Call	80	8:1	88	7:1 '√'
3. Second Meeting and Demo	19	4:1	15	6:1 'X'
4.				
5.				
6.				
7.				
8.				
Revenue Achieved	$95K	N/A	$86K 'X'	N/A

Above we see some sample data for one month. Starting at the bottom we can see that you didn't make your target. But why? Instantly, by using ratios you can see that you did really well in converting cold calls to meetings – much better than expected. (NOTE: For this example, I have used 'X' and '√' to denote over/under target – normally colours (like green/red) would highlight the status). BUT, you did a lot less of them than you could have. There's one issue identified. Then, you moved far less of them on to the 2nd stage than you normally achieve. What has happened? A more active competitor with an offer? Less marketplace interest? What was not resonating in that first meeting? You can dig right into what is happening – almost in real time, in order to get early warning, change tactics or focus on one problem stage when you have this data...

This is almost impossible to do when you don't have that simple clarity of measure and analysis. Ratios work! And it's easy to do...

Appendix 4

Some more words on the theories
and individuals quoted in the book

As I wrote this book I thought of a number of people and ideas that had influenced me over the years. Several of them made it into the final product. So, here is some more information on a few of them. Of course, as always today, you can dig much deeper yourself, if you want to, by pulling up Google or YouTube. All of the descriptions below are mine. Any errors, over-simplifications or misunderstandings are entirely my own!

So, in no particular order of importance –

Pavlov – Chapter 15
He of the famous dog experiment. Pavlov is known worldwide for his testing and what he found about defining and modifying behaviour. I P Pavlov developed a theory of 'conditioning' in Behavioural Psychology. It was all about using a method to cause a reflex response or behaviour through repetition. His famous experiment was on dogs. He used a set of dogs and each time, just before he fed them, he rang a bell. After some time, the dogs actually reacted physically – by salivating – when they heard the bell alone. Thus 'Pavlov's Dogs'. He proved the theory but I am sure you can all think of examples that impact you. Do certain adverts on the TV make you want something? You have just experienced Pavlovian Conditioning!

Herb Cohen – Chapter 7
One of my favourite speakers. Probably the world's best-known negotiator. Perhaps his biggest claim to fame was being brought in by the US government to help them in the Iran Hostage Crisis negotiations – presumably because no one in the government could negotiate as well as he did! He is a prolific writer and a serial interviewee – you can find lots on him on YouTube. His ideas, approach and books are superb.

Primacy and Recency – Chapter 14
This comes under the broader 'Serial-Position Effect' (Hermann Ebbinghaus). This is a widely tested and quoted

effect within the teaching of Psychology. At its simplest (so I can understand it) the message is really straightforward. In any order of things that you try to remember, the first and last in that series (demonstrations, interviewees, adverts etc) are always the ones that come to mind the most easily – hence Primacy and Recency.

Four Stages of Teams – Chapter 16
Bruce Tuckman introduced this concept which is now widely used in Management Training programmes. The four stages – Forming, Storming, Norming and Performing – simply denote the evolution of a team as it develops and the dynamics of that process. Google brought up 133 million reference articles on this one!

Stew Leonards – Chapter 17
One of the best business stories of all time. Starting off as a small 'dairy store' in 1969, the company now has 6 stores and 2,000 employees. They created that wonderful quote now used all around the world as the definition of their business approach – *"Rule number 1. The customer is always right. Rule number 2. If the customer is ever wrong, re-read rule number 1".* This statement is etched on a 3-ton granite stone outside each store. Go online to their website or Google to find out more about this unique – and incredibly successful – business.

Myers Briggs
The world's most widely used – and accepted – personality testing process. In the 1920s Katharine Briggs and Isabel Myers studied the works of Carl Jung. In the 1940s they developed a set of standard tests to help organisations and individuals understand and classify personality types. In 1962 the first publication of the MBTI Manual was released. This document was used for further research until 1977. In 1984 the Myers & Briggs Foundation was established. This has led to the large number of subsequent and/or similar 'do it yourself' tests to be found online (25.5 million as I type this) if you just enter 'Myers Briggs'. Very enlightening!

Maslow's Hierarchy of Needs – Chapter 19
Abraham Maslow introduced this concept in 1943. It tells us about a pyramid of needs we all have (5 levels in all). The base is the fundamental requirements for life and the higher ones are about things like esteem and love/belonging.

Thanks to the 'verywellmind' website for this great summary.
"Maslow's hierarchy is most often displayed as a pyramid. The lowest levels of the pyramid are made up of the most basic needs, while the most complex needs are at the top of the pyramid.

Needs at the bottom of the pyramid are basic physical requirements including the need for food, water, sleep, and warmth. Once these lower-level needs have been met, people can move on to the next level of needs, which are for safety and security.

As people progress up the pyramid, needs become increasingly psychological and social. Soon, the need for love, friendship, and intimacy become important. Further up the pyramid, the need for personal esteem and feelings of accomplishment take priority."

Versions of the Hierarchy also exist for use in the business world. The equivalent levels in these hierarchies talk about job security, becoming part of a team, achieving targets etc.

KEEP LEARNING!

Look out for the follow up book

...coming later in 2020!

Made in the USA
Coppell, TX
09 October 2024